Seven Strategies
of Assessment *for* Learning

Seven Strategies
of Assessment *for* Learning

Jan Chappuis

Educational Testing Service
Portland, Oregon ■ Princeton, New Jersey

Cover design: Clara Sue Beym

Book design and typesetting: Curtis Bay and Heidi Bay, Grey Sky Design

Editing: Robert L. Marcum, editorbob.com

Project Coordination: Barbara Fankhauser

Educational Testing Service
317 SW Alder Street, Suite 1200
Portland, OR 97204

Printed in the U.S.A.

ISBN 978-0-88685-401-0

Library of Congress Pre-assigned Control Number (PNC): 2008924607

Preface

When I began teaching in 1978, I remember walking around my fourth-grade classroom and thinking, "I can't believe they pay me to do this job." I liked everything about it, except grading. I could not make peace with that part of the job—it felt like I was giving with the teaching hand and taking away with the grading hand. Some of what I did then, and later as a secondary school teacher, was unfair to students, partly because I didn't know how to assess accurately, and partly because I didn't know how to do anything with assessment but grade.

My introduction to assessment *for* learning came in the summer of 1981 as a participant in the Puget Sound Writing Project, where I learned to revise my own writing based on thoughtful feedback from colleagues and to reflect on myself as a writer. I brought back to my classroom a writing-process approach, where students had opportunities to draft and revise, to give and respond to feedback before submitting their work for a grade. These practices significantly improved both the quality of their writing and their attitude toward it. My interest in assessment's formative classroom potential grew from that experience.

During the 1980s I studied feedback, self-assessment, self-reflection, and metacognition. Like many teachers before me and since, I experimented with devising lessons and activities using these ideas to deepen students' understanding of the content and of themselves as learners. I drew ideas from the work of Grant Wiggins, Rick Stiggins, and Vicki Spandel, all advocates of using assessment to advance, not merely measure, achievement. As I moved from the classroom into curriculum development and then to staff development, I focused my work with teachers on assessment practices that help students learn.

The seven strategies I describe in this book represent a synthesis of best thinking in the field. They've been shaped by thirty years of teaching, reading, experimenting, and learning from students and colleagues, and refined through hundreds of presentations I've given over the years to school faculties.

Since 2001, my husband Steve and I have worked with Rick Stiggins and Judy Arter at the ETS Assessment Training Institute in Portland, Oregon. Collectively and in various combinations, the four of us have written a series of books aimed at improving teachers' classroom assessment practice. Our primary text, *Classroom Assessment for Student Learning: Doing It Right—Using It Well* (known as *CASL*), published in 2004, is grounded in the concept of student-involved assessment. In it, we introduced the seven strategies of assessment *for* learning. With the help of colleagues and friends, this book extends those ideas into practical applications.

Acknowledgements

In writing this book, I am indebted to many for their ideas, talents, and assistance: teacher Bud Creighton, for insight into the power of noticing student success; teacher Claudia Rengstorf, for showing what students are capable of doing when we move from the front of the classroom to the side; writer Vicki Spandel, for her pioneering of assessment *for* learning strategies in teaching and assessing writing; colleagues Judy Arter, Steve Chappuis, and Rick Stiggins, from whom I have learned so much and with whom I am honored to continue learning; office staff Jennifer Cavanagh, Shannon Howland, and Iwona Kiebasinski for their research and editing skills, clerical expertise, and overall alacrity; project manager Barbara Fankhauser for gently shepherding the book-making process from outline to final printing; editor Robert L. Marcum for his gift of clarity, commitment to quality in the details, and overall dedication to this project; designers Heidi Bay and Curtis Bay for their ability to enhance meaning visually and their good-natured spirit through many trials; and to my husband Steve and daughter Claire for their love, understanding, and cheerful willingness to both work and play without me during the writing of this book. Lastly, I am grateful to the hundreds of teachers and administrators who sent examples of how they are using the seven strategies in their classrooms and districts. This book is richer for their work. Thank you all.

Jan Chappuis
Portland, Oregon
February 2009

Table of Contents

CHAPTER 1

Formative Assessment and Assessment *for* Learning

> Innovations that include strengthening the practice of
> formative assessment produce significant and often
> substantial learning gains.
>
> —*Black & Wiliam, 1998b, p. 140*

*T*his conclusion, from Paul Black and Dylan Wiliam's comprehensive review of research on formative assessment practices, has changed the face of assessment today. It is in large part responsible for the widespread focus in education on the particular kind of assessment known as "formative."

Their research review (1998a) examined studies that collectively encompassed kindergarteners to college students; represented a range of subject areas including reading, writing, social studies, mathematics, and science; and were conducted in numerous countries throughout the world, including the United States. The gains reported in the studies they describe are among the largest found for any educational intervention.

Typical effect sizes were between 0.4 and 0.7. In other words, the achievement gains realized by students whose teachers rely on formative assessment can range from 15 to 25 percentile points, or two to four grade equivalents, on commonly used standardized achievement test score scales. In broader terms, this kind of score gain, if applied to performance on recent international assessments, would move the United States's rank from the middle of the pack of 42 nations tested to the top five (Black & Wiliam, 1998b).

An additional outcome common among the studies they analyzed is that certain formative assessment practices greatly increased the achievement of low-performing students, in some cases to the point of approaching that of high-achieving students. Not surprisingly, a plethora of formative assessment programs and products has surfaced, due in part to the achievement gains and gap-closing powers reported by Black and Wiliam and other researchers. The adjective *formative* now appears frequently in titles of commercially prepared tests and item banks, interim and benchmark tests, short-cycle assessments, and classroom assessments.

Does calling a product or practice "formative" make it so? Are all of the tests and practices labeled as "formative" truly formative? And most importantly, what is it about *formative* that gives it its power? What led to the gains these researchers uncovered?

What Is Formative Assessment?

First let's look at what is and what isn't formative. For Black and Wiliam, and for many other experts in the field, formative assessment is not an *instrument* or an *event*, but a collection of practices with a common feature: *they all lead to some action that improves learning*. Well-known educational researchers emphasize this point when they describe what is at the heart of formative assessment:

> "Formative assessment, therefore, is essentially feedback (Ramaprasad, 1983) both to the teachers and to the pupil about present understanding and skill development in order to determine the way forward" (Harlen & James, 1997, p. 369).

> "[Formative assessment] refers to assessment that is specifically intended to provide feedback on performance to improve and accelerate learning" (Sadler, 1998, p. 77).

> "An assessment is formative to the extent that information from the assessment is fed back within the system and actually used to improve the performance of the system in some way" (Wiliam & Leahy, 2007, p. 31).

> "Formative assessment is defined as assessment carried out during the instructional process for the purpose of improving teaching or learning. . . . What makes formative assessment formative is that it is immediately used to make adjustments so as to form new learning" (Shepard, 2008, p. 281).

The common thread woven throughout formative assessment research, articles, and books bears repeating: it is *not the instrument* that is formative; it is the *use of the information* gathered, by whatever means, *to adjust teaching and learning*, that merits the "formative" label (Figure 1.1).

Figure 1.1

Formative Assessment
Formal and informal processes teachers and students use to gather evidence for the purpose of improving learning

In the classroom we assess formally through assignments, tests, quizzes, performances, projects, and surveys; or informally through questioning and dialogue, observing, and anecdotal note taking. In any of these instances, we may or may not be engaged in formative assessment: the determining factor is not the type of assessment we use, but rather how we and our students use the information.

Summative Assessment

When the information from an assessment is used solely to make a judgment about level of competence or achievement, it is a *summative assessment* (Figure 1.2). At the classroom level, an assessment is summative when it is given to determine how much students have learned at a particular point in time, for the purpose of communicating achievement status to others. The communication

Figure 1.2

Summative Assessment
Assessments that provide evidence of student achievement for the purpose of making a judgment about student competence or program effectiveness

usually takes the form of a symbol, a letter grade or number, or a comparison to a standard such as "Meets the Standard" or "Proficient," that is reported to students and eventually to parents. Sometimes an assessment intended to be used formatively can be used summatively, such as when the evidence indicates that students have attained mastery. And sometimes an assessment intended to be used summatively can be used formatively, such as when a test reveals significant problems with learning that we address through reteaching.

At the program level, an assessment is summative when results are used to make judgments such as determining how many students are and are not meeting standards in a certain subject for purposes of accountability. The data may be reported to educators within the system, the school board, and the community.

Summative assessments aren't bad or wrong. They're just not formative; they have a different purpose—to report out level of achievement. Mislabeling them as *formative* will not cause them to generate the achievement gains noted in research studies.

Formative or Summative?

An important reason to distinguish between formative and summative assessment is that achievement gains credited to formative assessment practices will not materialize unless certain conditions are met, and at least some of these conditions are often *not* met by assessments whose primary purpose is summative. The conditions are as follows:

1. The assessment instrument or event is designed so that it aligns directly with the content standards to be learned.

2. All of the instrument or event's items or tasks match what has been or will be taught.

3. The instrument or event provides information of sufficient detail to pinpoint specific problems, such as misunderstandings, so that teachers can make good decisions about what actions to take, and with whom.

4. The results are available in time to take action with the students who generated them.

5. Teachers and students do indeed take action based on the results.

If one or more of these conditions is not fulfilled, it is at best an incomplete attempt, and at worst harmful to learning. If the intent is formative, but the use is summative, it is a wasted opportunity. Assessment does not accomplish a formative purpose when "the information is simply recorded, passed on to a third party who lacks either the knowledge or the power to change the outcome, or is too deeply coded (for example, as a summary grade given by the teacher) to lead to appropriate action" (Sadler, 1989, p. 121).

It is a good idea to review the assessments considered formative in your context against the requirements for effective formative use. You may also want to refer to the table in Figure 1.3, which lists types of assessments present in many current school systems, identifies their purposes, and classifies their intended uses.

What Gives Formative Assessment Its Power?

The collection of hundreds of studies Black & Wiliam (1998a, 1998b) examined represents a diverse array of interventions, all of which featured some formative use of assessment data or processes. Practices yielding the largest achievement gains displayed the following characteristics:

- Use of classroom discussions, classroom tasks, and homework to determine the current state of student learning/understanding, with action taken to improve learning/correct misunderstandings

- Provision of descriptive feedback, with guidance on how to improve, during the learning

- Development of student self- and peer-assessment skills

Drawing from their analysis of these studies, Black & Wiliam (1998b) make the following recommendations about key components of formative assessment:

- "Opportunities for students to express their understandings should be designed into any piece of teaching, for this will initiate the interaction through which formative assessment aids learning" (p. 143).

Figure 1.3

Formative or Summative?

Type of assessment	What is the purpose?	Who will use the information?	How will it be used?	Is the use formative or summative?
State test	Measure level of achievement on state content standards	State	Determine AYP	Summative
		District, Teacher Teams	Determine program effectiveness	Summative
	Identify percentage of students meeting performance standards on state content standards	State	Comparison of schools/districts	Summative
		District, Teacher Teams	Develop programs/interventions for groups or individuals	Formative
District bench-mark, interim, or common assessment	Measure level of achievement toward state content standards	District, Teacher Teams	Determine program effectiveness	Summative
		District, Teacher Teams	Identify program needs	Formative
	Identify students needing additional help	District, Teacher Teams, Teachers	Plan interventions for groups or individuals	Formative
Classroom assessment	Measure level of achievement on learning targets taught	Teachers	Determine report card grade	Summative
	Diagnose student strengths and areas needing reteaching	Teacher Teams, Teachers	Revise teaching plans for next year/semester	Formative
			Plan further instruction/ differentiate instruction for these students	Formative
		Teachers, Students	Provide feedback to students	Formative
	Understand strengths and areas needing work	Students	Self-assess, set goals for further study/work	Formative

Program = curriculum, texts/resources, and pedagogy
Identifying program needs:
Are we teaching to the right content standards/learning targets?
Do we have sufficient texts and other resources?
Are our teaching strategies effective?

- "The dialogue between pupils and teachers should be thoughtful, reflective, focused to evoke and explore understanding, and conducted so that all pupils have an opportunity to think and to express their ideas" (p. 144).

- "Feedback to any pupil should be about the particular qualities of his or her work, with advice on what he or she can do to improve, and should avoid comparison with other pupils" (p. 143).

- "Feedback on tests, seatwork, and homework should give each pupil guidance on how to improve, and each pupil must be given help and an opportunity to work on the improvement" (p.144).

- "If formative assessment is to be productive, pupils should be trained in self-assessment so that they can understand the main purposes of their learning and thereby grasp what they need to do to achieve" (p. 143).

Notice where these recommended practices fall on the chart in Figure 1.3. Formative assessment *is* a powerful tool in the hands of both teachers and students and the closer to everyday instruction, the stronger it is. Classroom assessment, sensitive to what teachers and students are doing daily, is most capable of providing the basis for understandable and accurate feedback about the learning, while there is still time to act on it. And it has the greatest capacity to develop students' ability to monitor and adjust their own learning.

Formative Assessment in Teachers' Hands

Many formative assessment strategies address the teacher's information needs, helping to answer questions critical to good instruction:

- Who is and is not understanding the lesson?

- What are this student's strengths and needs?

- What misconceptions do I need to address?

- What feedback should I give students?

- What adjustments should I make to instruction?

- How should I group students?

- What differentiation do I need to prepare?

There is no doubt that, acting on good information during the course of instruction, teachers can increase what and how well students learn. Indeed, some of the significant achievement gains attributable to formative assessment are due to enhanced questioning and dialogue techniques.

Many strong programs and practices help teachers obtain, interpret, and act on student achievement information. Data-driven decision making, developing interim assessments, Response to Intervention, differentiated instruction, minute-by-minute assessment, and questioning strategies are among the more well known of those focusing on teacher decision making. If you are already familiar with the term *formative assessment*, you probably have encountered its use in one or more of these contexts.

However, if teacher use of assessment information is our total picture of formative assessment, one very important player is sitting on the sidelines, and it's not the principal or the superintendent. We have benched the student.

Formative Assessment in Students' Hands

Black and Wiliam's (1998a) research review showcases the student as decision maker. Many other prominent education experts, such as Rick Stiggins, Lorrie Shepard, Grant Wiggins, Jay McTighe, and Sue Brookhart, have also described the benefits of student involvement in the assessment process. In an often-cited article describing how formative assessment improves achievement, Sadler (1989) concludes that it hinges on developing students' capacity to monitor the quality of their own work during production:

> "Whatever the procedures by which the assessment message is generated, it would be a mistake to regard the student as the passive recipient of a call to action."
>
> *Black & Wiliam, 1998a, p. 21*

> The indispensable conditions for improvement are that the *student* comes to hold a concept of quality roughly similar to that held by the teacher, is able to monitor continuously the quality of what is being produced *during the act of production itself*, and has a repertoire of alternative moves or strategies from which to draw at any given point. (p. 121, emphasis in original)

Writing about formative assessment in the science classroom, Atkin, Black, & Coffey (2001) translate the conditions Sadler describes into three questions:

1. Where are you trying to go? (identify and communicate the learning and performance goals);

2. Where are you now? (assess, or help the student to self-assess, current levels of understanding);

3. How can you get there? (help the student with strategies and skills to reach the goal). (p. 14)

Sadler's conditions as represented in these three questions frame what is called "Assessment *for* Learning"—formative assessment practices designed to meet students' information needs to maximize both motivation and achievement, by involving students from the start in their own learning (Stiggins, Arter, Chappuis, & Chappuis, 2004).

My colleagues and I at the ETS Assessment Training Institute have been developing classroom applications of assessment *for* learning over the past decade and have created a framework of seven strategies to organize assessment *for* learning practices focused on the needs of the learner.

Seven Strategies of Assessment *for* Learning

The seven strategies fulfill Sadler's three conditions, phrased as questions from the student's point of view: *Where am I going?*; *Where am I now?*; and *How can I close the gap?* As you read through these strategies, note that many are not new—they reflect practices that have been around for years (Figure 1.4). What may be new is their *intentional* use, focusing on the student as the most influential decision maker in your classroom.

Where Am I Going?

Strategy 1: Provide students with a clear and understandable vision of the learning target.
Motivation and achievement both increase when instruction is guided by clearly defined targets. Activities that help students answer the question, "What's the learning?" set the stage for all further formative assessment actions.

Figure 1.4

Seven Strategies of Assessment *for* Learning

Where Am I Going?

Strategy 1: Provide students with a clear and understandable vision of the learning target.

Strategy 2: Use examples and models of strong and weak work.

Where Am I Now?

Strategy 3: Offer regular descriptive feedback.

Strategy 4: Teach students to self-assess and set goals.

How Can I Close the Gap?

Strategy 5: Design lessons to focus on one learning target or aspect of quality at a time.

Strategy 6: Teach students focused revision.

Strategy 7: Engage students in self-reflection, and let them keep track of and share their learning.

Source: Adapted with permission from R. J. Stiggins, J. A. Arter, J. Chappuis, and S. Chappuis, *Classroom Assessment* for *Student Learning: Doing It Right—Using It Well* (Portland, OR: ETS Assessment Training Institute, 2004), p. 42.

Strategy 2: Use examples and models of strong and weak work.

Carefully chosen examples of the range of quality can create and refine students' understanding of the learning goal by helping students answer the questions, "What defines quality work?" and "What are some problems to avoid?"

Where Am I Now?

Strategy 3: Offer regular descriptive feedback.

Effective feedback shows students where they are on their path to attaining the intended learning. It answers for students the questions, "What are my strengths?"; "What do I need to work on?"; and "Where did I go wrong and what can I do about it?"

Strategy 4: Teach students to self-assess and set goals.

The information provided in effective feedback models the kind of evaluative thinking we want students to be able to do themselves. Strategy 4 teaches students to identify their strengths and weaknesses and to set goals for further learning. It helps them answer the questions, "What am I good at?"; "What do I need to work on?"; and "What should I do next?"

How Can I Close the Gap?

Strategy 5: Design lessons to focus on one learning target or aspect of quality at a time.

When assessment information identifies a need, we can adjust instruction to target that need. In this strategy, we scaffold learning by narrowing the focus of a lesson to help students master a specific learning goal or to address specific misconceptions or problems.

Strategy 6: Teach students focused revision.

This is a companion to Strategy 5—when a concept, skill, or competence proves difficult for students, we can let them practice it in smaller segments, and give them feedback on just the aspects they are practicing. This strategy allows students to revise their initial work with a focus on a manageable number of learning targets or aspects of quality.

Strategy 7: Engage students in self-reflection, and let them keep track of and share their learning.

Long-term retention and motivation increase when students track, reflect on, and communicate about their learning. In this strategy, students look back on their journey, reflecting on their learning and sharing their achievement with others.

The seven strategies are not a recipe to be followed step by step, although they do build on one another. Rather, they are a collection of actions that will strengthen students' sense of self-efficacy (belief that effort will lead to improvement), their motivation to try, and ultimately, their achievement. They represent a use of assessment information that differs from the traditional practice of associating *assessment* with *test*, and *test* with *grade*. These assessment practices will not result in more grades in the gradebook. Rather, they ask us to think more broadly about what assessment is and what it is capable of accomplishing.

Conclusion

These activities won't eliminate the achievement gap in your classroom. Too many factors are at work to be completely overcome by one set of strategies. However, they will take you farther in that direction by helping you reclaim assessment as an integral part of teaching and learning. The Seven Strategies of Assessment *for* Learning offer a sequence of effective research-based practices that develop in students the patterns of thought they need to substantially improve their own achievement, and in doing so, they will introduce your students to the motivational power of being in control of the conditions of their success. Assessment can be your friend—it can even be fun. And it can be your students' friend, too.

The Chapters Ahead

The remaining chapters will explain the strategies in detail, provide a research-based rationale for their use, describe how they work and offer hands-on classroom activities that you can use tomorrow. Each chapter includes instructions for carrying out core procedures and suggestions for adaptations, all selected to make the intent and the execution of the strategy as clear as possible. Examples come from pre-kindergarten to college levels in a range of content areas. The majority can be adapted to work well in most contexts. Even if an example is not from your grade level or subject, try not to ignore it. You will find information about key research recommendations that will help you easily modify the ideas to fit your context without diluting their potential for positive impact.

Appendix A contains three student-friendly rubrics referred to in the text, and Appendix B has reproducible versions of student forms presented in each of the chapters.

CHAPTER 2

Where Am I Going?
Clear Targets

Strategy 1
Provide students with a clear and understandable vision of the learning target.

Strategy 2
Use examples and models of strong and weak work.

Strategy 1

Provide students with a clear and understandable vision of the learning target.

Strategy 2

Use examples and models of strong and weak work.

> Involving pupils in their own assessment means that they must know what are the aims of their learning. Communicating these aims is not easy, but the rewards of successfully attempting it are quite considerable, not only for help in assessment, but also in the obvious potential for self-direction in learning.
>
> —*Harlen & James, 1997, p. 372*

*T*aken together, Strategy 1 and Strategy 2 develop in students an internal vision of what they are to be learning. When we invest time up front to build the vision, we gain it back later in increased student motivation and the resulting higher-quality work.

These two strategies act as "enabling strategies," setting the stage for Strategies 3 and 4: feedback, self-assessment, and goal setting. The role of feedback is to show students where they are now with respect to where they are headed, to diagnose and prescribe; if students don't have a clear vision of their destination, feedback does not hold much meaning for them. Good self-assessment mirrors good feedback; the student is *self*-diagnosing and *self*-prescribing. Self-assessment, Black and William (1998a) note, is the indispensable condition for effective learning (p. 25), and it cannot be done well without accurate understanding of the

"There is a diagnostic aspect to all formative assessment, and diagnostic information can inform both students' studying and teachers' teaching. The key is having a concept of the goal or learning target, which originally is the teacher's, but which ideally the student will internalize, eventually setting his or her own goals and monitoring progress toward them (Sadler, 1989; Gipps, 1994)."

Brookhart, 2001, p. 154

intended learning goal. While it may be tempting to regard these first two strategies as less important than other assessment *for* learning practices, they are essential to the development of students' capabilities as self-reliant learners.

Ask a student what she *learned* today, and it's possible she'll draw a blank. She may tell you what she *did* ("We worked on a math problem about camping," or "We watched our teacher cook stuff and then we got to eat it"), but she may not be able to tell you why. This student's attention is not focused on what it is she is supposed to be learning—it is focused on what she is doing. In other words, she has a performance goal, rather than a learning goal. There is a body of research that indicates that when students are given *learning goals*, goals that describe the intended learning, they perform significantly better than students who are given *performance goals*, goals that focus on task completion (Black & Wiliam, 1998a; Shepard, 2001). When a student believes his job today is to learn how to use the strategy "draw a picture" to solve math problems, he has a learning goal. When he thinks his job today is to solve a set of problems, he has a performance goal. If a student believes her job in chemistry is to pay attention while the teacher toasts bread, makes salad dressing, and bakes cookies, she has a performance goal. If she believes her job is to draw inferences about the differences between a physical and a chemical change, she has a learning goal. Making the intended learning clear to students substitutes a learning-goal orientation for their activity-oriented, performance-goal way of thinking. It focuses their attention on learning by helping them understand the assignment is the *means* and the learning is the *end*.

Before sharing learning targets with our students, we need to make sure they are clear to us. If, for example, your content standards are written in the form of benchmarks, you may need to "unpack" them—to tease out the collection of learning targets that represents the intent of the benchmark. Figure 2.1 shows a high school biology teacher's translation of benchmarks into learning targets that guide his instruction. Figure 2.2 offers guidance on clarifying learning targets.

Communicating learning goals can be as simple as sharing the intended learning for the lesson—"Today we're going to learn how to read decimals to the tenths place and put them in order." Or it can be more complex, as when converting a rubric for scientific inquiry into student-friendly language and then teaching students what it means. It can take from five seconds to several weeks, depending on the complexity and importance of the learning target, and the age of your students. In this chapter, we'll focus on a spectrum of activities you can use to make "Where am I going?" clear to students.

Figure 2.1

FOR EXAMPLE

Unpacking Biology Benchmarks

Describe the structures of viruses and bacteria

The word "describe" in this objective is tricky. Do they really want students to *describe* a capsid or flagellum? Or do they want them to identify structures on a diagram (a vastly more probable assessment)? I expect the students to be able to identify basic bacterial and viral structures on a simple diagram. To ensure that the benchmark is covered as completely as possible, they also need to describe the function of several structures as well. As written, this is knowledge/understanding. They should also use this information to compare and contrast the two. (Most students think they are the same thing.)

Recognize that while viruses lack cellular structure, they have genetic material to invade living cells

The reading of the benchmark is the teaching of it. This objective is, in a peripheral way, addressing the notion of whether or not viruses are alive. While they do not possess every characteristic of life (a requirement to be considered alive by the standard definition), they do have characteristics that are distinctly lifelike (specifically genetic material). Modern science does not have a consensus on this issue, so it lends itself well to having students evaluate the problem and propose a solution. This benchmark is knowledge/understanding, but the analysis of the life status of viruses is reasoning.

Relate cell parts/organelles to their function (limited by clarification document to cell membrane, cell wall, chloroplast, Golgi apparatus, mitochondria, nucleus, ribosome, and vacuole)

This benchmark is knowledge/understanding. It asks students to effectively define a variety of cell structures. Later in the class, students are expected to be able to connect the functions of the organelles to each other and to the processes we learn later on. For now, simple definitions are sufficient.

Compare and contrast plant and animal cells

This is the first objective in this unit that explicitly requires reasoning. Primarily, students are expected to list the organelles specific to plants and animals. In some cases, they may be expected to explain why the cells differ (for example: why don't animals have cell walls or why do plants have larger vacuoles?).

Source: Used with permission from Andy Hamilton, unpublished classroom materials, West Ottawa Public Schools, Holland, MI, 2008.

Figure 2.2

Prerequisite: Clear Targets

You can't make targets clear to students if they aren't clear to you. Let's say that the clearest target your curriculum document gives you is not clear enough to guide your teaching focus. Either you and your colleagues agree that it is not specific enough to know what to teach and assess, or you interpret it differently among you, so that students in various classrooms will be experiencing significantly different learning. This can happen when some teachers interpret a learning target as calling for knowledge-level learning and others think it calls for something beyond knowledge—some form of reasoning or skill demonstration. Take, for example, "Knows how to measure cardio respiratory fitness." Does this mean "Can repeat the steps in measuring cardio respiratory fitness" or "Measures own cardio respiratory fitness accurately"? It is likely that the two interpretations will lead to different sets of classroom experiences and ultimate assessment.

When learning targets begin with the word "Understands," such as "Understands the concept of diversity," you and your colleagues must decide how you will define *understands* in this context and at your grade level. Will you ask students to define the concept as the ultimate learning or to go beyond the knowledge/recall level to do something with the concept? If you choose "go beyond," you will need to specify what pattern of reasoning (compare and contrast? analyze and draw conclusions? evaluate?) will take the concept out of the land of recall.

Sometimes learning targets are stated as benchmarks, which may need to be "unpacked." In this case, you create a list of learning targets inherent in the intent of each benchmark, as illustrated in Figure 2.1. For more information on unpacking benchmarks, see Stiggins et al., 2004, Chapter 3.

If your learning targets are clear but complex, you can break them down into manageable, teachable chunks. For example, you may have a science content standard that states, "Plans and conducts a simple investigation." In this case, you and your colleagues may decide to break the target into two stages— teaching students how to plan an investigation, and then teaching them the skills and protocols they will need to carry out the investigation. Each of these

Figure 2.2 (continued)

stages can be lengthy and complex in themselves. Your curriculum guide may offer more specificity:

- Make predictions of the results of an investigation.
- Generate a logical plan for, and conduct, a simple controlled investigation with the following attributes:
    —Prediction
    —Appropriate materials, tools, and available computer technology
    —Variables kept the same (controlled)
    —One changed variable (manipulated)
    —Measured (responding) variable
    —Multiple trials
- Gather, record, and organize data using appropriate units, charts, and/or graphs.
- Generate a logical plan for a simple field investigation showing the following steps:
    —Identify multiple variables.
    —Select observable or measurable variables related to the investigative question.
    —Identify and use simple equipment and tools (such as magnifiers, rulers, balances, scales, and thermometers) to gather data and extend the senses.
    —Follow all safety rules during investigations.

Now you have something specific enough to work with.

Source: Adapted from "K–10 Grade Level Expectations: A New Level of Specificity. Washington State's Essential Academic Learning Requirements" (Olympia, WA: Office of Superintendent of Public Instruction, 2005). Retrieved 20 September 2008 from http://www.k12.wa.us/curriculumInstruct/science/pubdocs/ScienceEALR-GLE.pdf

Strategy 1: Provide students with a clear and understandable vision of the learning target.

Sharing learning targets with students can play out in several ways depending on the kind of target (knowledge, reasoning, performance skill, or product) and its complexity. Some learning targets are clear enough to be stated to students in their original form—"Today, we're learning how to prepare microscope slides." Other targets, while clear to you, may not be clear to students, so you may want to translate them into student-friendly terms.

For *knowledge* and some *reasoning* targets—those you can assess using selected response or short-answer formats—you can create a student-friendly definition. For other *reasoning* targets, as well as *performance skill* and *product* targets—those you will assess with performance assessment—you will need to find or create a student-friendly rubric. (For more information on kinds of learning targets and their match to assessment methods, see Stiggins et al., 2004, Chapters 3 & 4.)

Converting Knowledge and Reasoning Learning Targets to Student-friendly Language

Consider the reading learning target, "Summarizes what is read." Does every student who reads that phrase know what it means to summarize? If the summaries your students write are almost as long as the passage itself, you can be sure they have misconstrued the essence of "summarize." This is an example of a target that can be clarified by creating a student-friendly definition.

Figure 2.3

Making Targets Clear to Students

Provide a clear and understandable vision of the learning target.

- Share the learning target with students.

- Use language students understand.

- Introduce students to the language and concepts of the rubrics you use.

Here is a process you can use to turn learning targets into statements that your students will understand. Begin by selecting a target for which this is a good idea. Which knowledge and reasoning targets do students have difficulty with? It may be useful to check for understanding with students—what do they think it means? If they are clear, you don't have to translate the target. This process takes a little time, so choose with care. Remember, not all content standards need to be translated. ("We are learning to use a balance beam to weigh things accurately" works fine as is.)

Consult Your Curriculum

Consult your own curriculum documents when creating student-friendly definitions to ensure that your interpretations represent the intent of the content standards you are translating.

1. Identify the word(s) and/or phrase(s) needing clarification. Which terms will students struggle with? Imagine stating the target in its original form to your class. Then envision the degree of understanding reflected on faces throughout the room. At which word did they lose meaning?

2. Define the term(s) you have identified. Use a dictionary, your textbook, your state content standards document, or other reference materials specific to your subject. If you are working with a colleague, come to agreement on definitions.

3. Convert the definition(s) into language your students are likely to understand.

4. Turn the student-friendly definition into an "I" or a "We" statement: "I am learning to_____"; or "We are learning to _____." Run it by a colleague for feedback.

5. Try the definition out with students. Note their response. Refine as needed.

6. Let students have a go at this procedure occasionally, using learning targets you think they could successfully define and paraphrase. Make sure the definition they concoct is congruent with your vision of the target.

Figure 2.4 shows an example of this process applied to the second-grade learning target, "Makes inferences from informational/expository and literary/narrative text."

Figure 2.4

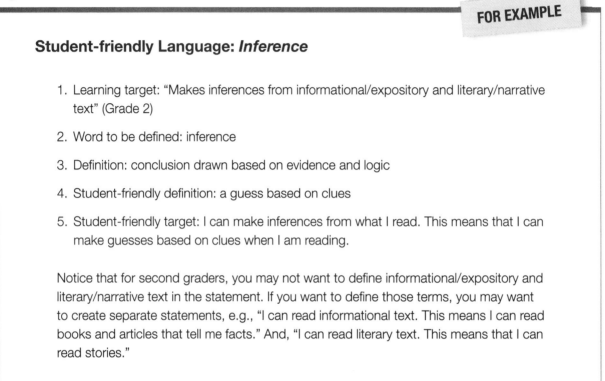

FOR EXAMPLE

Student-friendly Language: *Inference*

1. Learning target: "Makes inferences from informational/expository and literary/narrative text" (Grade 2)

2. Word to be defined: inference

3. Definition: conclusion drawn based on evidence and logic

4. Student-friendly definition: a guess based on clues

5. Student-friendly target: I can make inferences from what I read. This means that I can make guesses based on clues when I am reading.

Notice that for second graders, you may not want to define informational/expository and literary/narrative text in the statement. If you want to define those terms, you may want to create separate statements, e.g., "I can read informational text. This means I can read books and articles that tell me facts." And, "I can read literary text. This means that I can read stories."

The second example, Figure 2.5, defines a middle school reasoning learning target: "Generalizes information beyond the text." Although the context here is language arts, this reasoning proficiency plays an important role in other subjects such as mathematics, social studies, and science. It is a good idea to work with your colleagues in other content areas when you are translating reasoning learning targets to student-friendly language; most patterns of reasoning are used across disciplines and having a common definition for each benefits everyone who expects students to learn how to do it or demonstrate it.

Teachers of younger students may want to use a combination of words and pictures to make the meaning of the targets clear to them. Figure 2.6 shows an example of kindergarten music targets written this way.

You can also let students discuss the meaning of a learning target and write it in terms that are clear to them. This can work as a quick "anticipatory set" activity

Figure 2.5

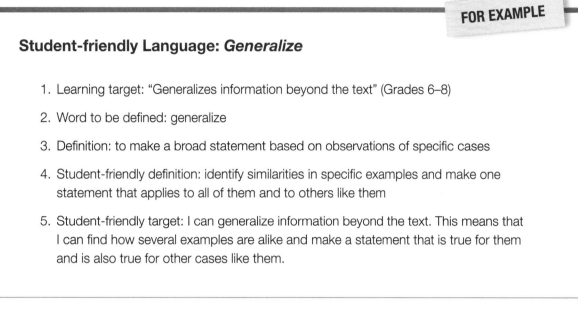

FOR EXAMPLE

Student-friendly Language: *Generalize*

1. Learning target: "Generalizes information beyond the text" (Grades 6–8)

2. Word to be defined: generalize

3. Definition: to make a broad statement based on observations of specific cases

4. Student-friendly definition: identify similarities in specific examples and make one statement that applies to all of them and to others like them

5. Student-friendly target: I can generalize information beyond the text. This means that I can find how several examples are alike and make a statement that is true for them and is also true for other cases like them.

or it can be the focus of an in-depth exploration. For example, middle school language arts teacher Jessica Cynkar has her students record the "adult" version of the indicator (learning target) they will be working on in their writing journals. They discuss in small groups what they think the indicator means and she then facilitates a whole-class discussion to create one common definition.

If you are working with benchmarks that you have unpacked, the list of learning targets you created can form the basis for student-friendly targets you give students. For example, biology teacher Andy Hamilton has his students record the daily objectives in a weekly log, which typically look like "I can" statements, but without the "I can" (for brevity). Figure 2.7 shows how he has unpacked two benchmarks into learning targets and then turned them into student-friendly statements.

When Not to Convert the Language

For some content standards, defining all of the terms will derail the learning, and so is not a good idea, even if students do not understand the vocabulary at the outset. Take for example the learning target, "Understands literary devices." You can list the literary devices they will be learning—similes, metaphors, alliteration, onomatopoeia, and so forth—but the point of the learning is that they be able to define them and locate them. So the student-friendly

 Use Professional Judgment

Not every learning target needs to be translated into student-friendly language. And learning targets don't always have to be shared at the outset of the lesson.

Figure 2.6

FOR EXAMPLE

Student-friendly Learning Targets for Kindergarten Music

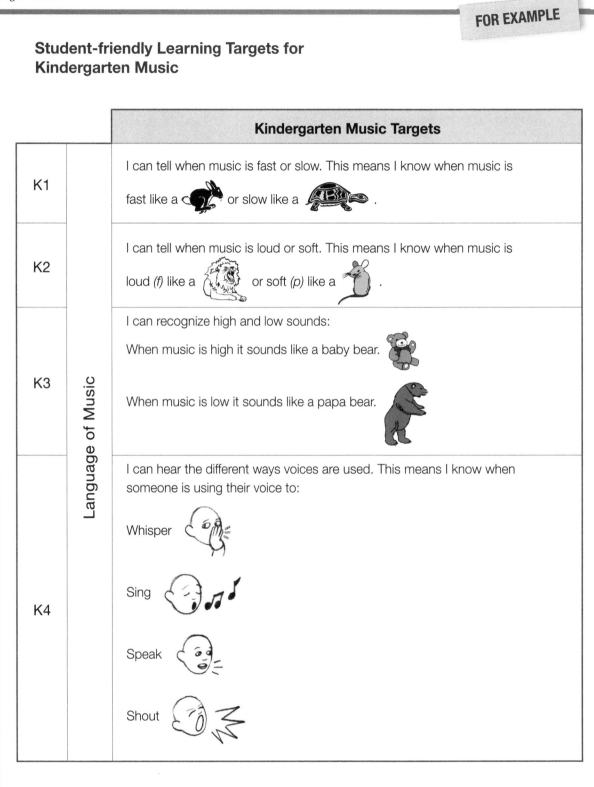

		Kindergarten Music Targets
K1		I can tell when music is fast or slow. This means I know when music is fast like a or slow like a .
K2	Language of Music	I can tell when music is loud or soft. This means I know when music is loud *(f)* like a or soft *(p)* like a .
K3		I can recognize high and low sounds: When music is high it sounds like a baby bear. When music is low it sounds like a papa bear.
K4		I can hear the different ways voices are used. This means I know when someone is using their voice to: Whisper Sing Speak Shout

Source: Used with permission from Jill Meciej, Community Consolidated School District 93, Bloomington, IL, 2008.

Figure 2.7

Benchmarks → Learning Targets → Student-friendly Targets

Benchmark: Explain that some structures in the modern eukaryotic cell developed from early prokaryotes, such as mitochondria, and in plants, chloroplasts

Learning Targets: The wording of this objective implies knowledge/understanding. In fact, reading the objective effectively teaches it to you. I expect my students to explain a little more about how those structures developed. This objective requires an understanding of the vocabulary terms *prokaryote* and *eukaryote* primarily, with *mitochondria* and *chloroplasts* being secondary vocabulary terms (you don't actually need to know what a chloroplast or mitochondrion is to learn the objective). Students should be able to describe the pieces of evidence that lead scientists to the conclusion that the objective is true.

Student-friendly Targets:

- I can define *prokaryote* and *eukaryote* and give examples of each.

- I can describe where mitochondria and chloroplasts come from.

- I can describe the evidence that explains where mitochondria and chloroplasts come from.

Benchmark: Explain the role of cell membranes as a highly selective barrier (diffusion, osmosis, and active transport)

Learning Targets: If you were to limit the scope of this objective to only what is written, students would simply have to describe that cell membranes are selective—that is, they let some things in and out but not others. I expect my students to do a lot more with this objective. They should be able to distinguish between types of membrane transport and describe what would happen in a variety of scenarios. As written, the benchmark is knowledge/understanding, but it lends itself well to reasoning and product learning targets.

Student-friendly Targets:

- I can define *osmosis*, *diffusion*, and *active transport*.

- I can predict what will happen when cells are placed in a variety of solutions.

- I can determine if a process is *osmosis*, *diffusion*, or *active transport* based on how materials are moving into or out of a cell.

Source: Used with permission from Andy Hamilton, unpublished classroom materials, West Ottawa Public Schools, Holland, MI, 2008.

version could sound something like, "We are learning to identify similes and metaphors in what we read." Another example is the learning target, "Understands the binomial theorem." You may want to define what "understand" will look like: Identify it? Define it? Explain it? Know when to use it? However, even though they don't know what the binomial theorem is at the outset, that is the heart of the learning, so in this case, you would leave the phrase "binomial theorem" alone. The rule of thumb here is: Will a student-friendly definition point the way to success without giving away the store?

"I can . . ." or *"I am learning to . . ."*

Instead of "I can . . ." statements, some teachers like to phrase the targets students are working on as "We are learning to . . ." (or "I am learning to . . .") statements. When students have demonstrated evidence of mastery for the target, they convert it into an "I can . . ." statement, staple it to the evidence, and place it in a folder they can use when sharing what they have learned. This idea is explained more fully in Chapter 6.

Defining Quality for Reasoning, Performance Skill, and Product Learning Targets

In general, more complex reasoning targets, performance skill targets, and product targets are most accurately measured with essay or performance assessments: you assign a task in which students create an artifact or performance and you evaluate what they create or do using a scoring rubric that describes the features of quality you are looking for. For these targets, it is not so important that they be translated into student-friendly terms—what is important is that the version of the *scoring rubric* you use is descriptive of quality and written using terms that students understand.

"Introducing students to the criteria by which their work will be evaluated enables students to better understand the characteristics of good performance."

White & Frederiksen, 1998, p. 28

Many research studies focus on the positive effects of sharing the scoring rubric with students in advance of completing the assessment task, especially for lower-achieving students. Studies Black and Wiliam (1998a) cite as evidence of the impact of formative assessment on student achievement include the practice of teaching students the criteria by which their work would be judged. In Chapters 3 and 4, you will read about White and Frederiksen's (1998) findings on the achievement effects of peer- and self-assessment with a rubric. In an assessment *for* learning environment, students become familiar with the content of the rubric at the outset of instruction.

It makes sense that if students are to be able to self-assess, they must first understand the concepts that define quality. A good assessment *for* learning rubric answers for students the question, "Where am I going?" by describing in specific terms the features of quality that you will be teaching them to produce. It includes descriptions of each feature from "just beginning" to "proficient" so that it can function as a diagnostic tool for you and them. It aligns what you are teaching about elements of quality with what you are providing feedback on and, when the time comes, with what counts for the grade. Figure 2.8 illustrates the alignment needed.

Figure 2.8

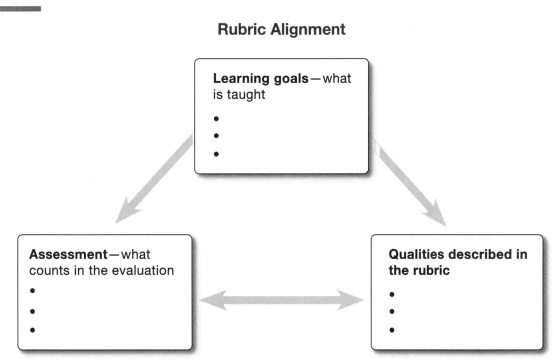

Rubric Alignment

Learning goals—what is taught
-
-
-

Assessment—what counts in the evaluation
-
-
-

Qualities described in the rubric
-
-
-

Developing a Student-friendly Rubric

Once you have found (or created) a suitable rubric you are ready to create a student-friendly version. Here are the steps in the process (Arter & Chappuis, 2006):

1. Identify the words and phrases in the adult version that your students might not understand.

2.   Look these words up in the dictionary or in textbooks. Discuss with colleagues the best phrasing choices for your students.

3.   Convert the definitions into wording your students will understand. Sometimes you need to convert one word into one or more phrases or sentences.

4.   Phrase the student-friendly version in the first person.

5.   Try the rubric out with students. Ask for their feedback.

6.   Revise as needed.

The two student-friendly versions of the mathematics problem-solving rubric in Appendix A were created using this process.

Introducing the Language of the Rubric to Students

Handing out a student-friendly rubric and going over it may not be the most effective way to introduce the concepts. In the following activity, you ask students what they already know about the characteristics of quality and then compare what they say to features the rubric describes, before distributing it. By doing this, you are accessing prior knowledge as well as generating some interest and motivation to pay attention to it.

Match to Targets

The content of your rubric should match your learning targets. When you are considering a rubric for possible use, ask yourself if it includes the dimensions you will be teaching. If not, revise the rubric or find a different one that matches the elements of quality you and your district, state, or province believe are important.

You will need copies of the rubric written in language your students will understand, and a list of the traits or criteria with brief descriptions of each. The example in Figure 2.9 is the list of criteria for the mathematics problem-solving rubric designed for third and fourth graders. The rubric has three traits, or criteria—three separate scoring scales. Each criterion is followed by a brief list of characteristics that help students understand its content.

To illustrate the process of introducing criteria to students, we will work with a math problem-solving example:

1.   Ask students what good math problem solving looks like. Record all responses on chart paper. Keep this list in their language—don't paraphrase it.

Figure 2.9

Mathematics Problem-solving Criteria

Mathematical Knowledge: Concepts and Procedures

- Understands the mathematical ideas and operations selected

- Performs appropriate computations

- Chooses the right operations and does them correctly

Problem Solving

- Translates the problem into mathematical terms

- Chooses or creates a strategy

- Uses a strategy to solve the problem

- Checks solution to make sure it makes sense in the problem

Mathematical Communication

- Explains the strategy and processes used

- Explains why what was done was done

- Explains why answer works

Source: Used with permission of Central Kitsap School District, Silverdale, WA, 2001.

2. Have them solve a multistep mathematics problem, one that requires reasoning, applying a strategy, and communicating about what they did.

3. Then ask students to think about what they tried to do while they were solving the problem—should other characteristics go on the list? Record what they say, using their language. Don't worry if extraneous ideas show up; just record what they say.

4. If time permits, keep the list open for a few days. Add to it as students practice problem solving with different examples. Or show two examples of anonymous student work at different levels

of quality on one of the problems they have solved and ask them to decide which is better. Add their reasons to the chart. You are ready to move to the next step when the list includes some of the features described by your rubric.

5. Tell students that this is a good list, and that they have done exactly what teachers and other content area experts do when they are creating a rubric to judge math problem solving. Tell them that their list includes many of the same characteristics on the experts' list.

6. Introduce the "expert" list by saying that the experts came up with lots of ideas just like they did. There were so many, they knew no one could keep all of them in their head at one time, so they grouped their ideas together into categories. We call the categories *criteria* or *traits*. Then show the list of criteria represented in your rubric. For this mathematics rubric, you would display the following categories:

   • Mathematical Knowledge: Concepts and Procedures

   • Problem Solving

   • Mathematical Communication

7. Then show a bulleted list of the main features of each criterion, as represented in the descriptors. The bulleted list for *Mathematical Knowledge: Concepts and Procedures* looks like this:

   • Understands the mathematical ideas and operations selected

   • Performs appropriate computations

   • Chooses the right operations and does them correctly

   While showing each criterion's list, ask students to check for a match to the class list. If they find one, write the criterion (e.g., *Concepts and Procedures*) next to the word or phrase on their chart. If there are no matches, tell students they will be learning more about that criterion (e.g., *Concepts and Procedures*) later. Do the same for all of the criteria in your rubric. In going through this process, students identify what they already know, link their descriptions of quality to the language of the scoring guide, and realize that the concepts on the rubric are not totally foreign to them.

8. Hand out a version of the rubric written in language your students will understand.

Protocol for Introducing Criteria to Younger Students

With primary students, when the learning is clearly developmental, you can modify the previous protocol by using the following series of lessons to introduce the concept of *criteria*, to help them develop criteria for key classroom behaviors, and then to introduce criteria you will be using to evaluate their learning.

Lesson 1: Introducing the Concept of Criteria.
In this first lesson, you will be introducing the word *criteria* and the idea that we make choices based on criteria (adapted with permission from Jill Meciej & Jerry O'Shea, personal communication, 2008).

 Examples from Grade Levels You Don't Teach

Try not to dismiss or skip over an example that applies to a grade level or subject you don't teach. Even though it is tailored to a specific context, chances are it will include ideas that you can modify to work with your students.

Key Understanding:
People use criteria to think about choices and to make decisions.

Materials:
- Read-aloud book about a family. The book should describe different aspects about the family such as members, home, and so forth. The family does not need to be human (e.g., Mercer Mayer stories).
- Three or more pictures of common pets (e.g., dog, cat, fish, gerbil, hamster, bird, snake). Choose animals so that some are more suited to this family than others.

Process:
Introduce the story by saying, "People make choices every day. How do people make *good* choices? We will talk about steps people use when they make choices. The first step many people make is thinking about what they want and don't want. For example, many families have pets. There are many different types of pets. How do families decide what type of pet they want? To make this choice a family needs to think about what would make a good pet for their home and family. What would a family need to think about to select the best pet for the family?"

Then say, "I am going to read a story to you about a family. When I finish reading we will talk about the family and what they might like or need to think about when they are choosing a pet (or adding another pet to their family)."

Make a chart listing the ideas students generate about what would make a good pet for the family from the read-aloud. Give it a title such as, "Criteria for Choosing a Pet for the _____ (family)." After the list is complete, show students the pictures of pets one at a time. Review the criteria list for each pet, asking students to decide whether each criterion is present.

Say, "Using our criteria for a good pet for the family, and our thinking about each pet, which pet would make the best pet for them?" Let students make a choice and give reasons why. Guide them to use the criteria list for their reasons.

Closure:

Say, "The ideas on the list we created and used to choose a pet are called *criteria*. People use criteria to help them make decisions or choices. We will use the word *criteria* all year as we talk about making good decisions or choices."

Lesson 2: Creating Criteria for Making Choices in Familiar Situations.
In this example, students work in small groups to generate criteria for making choices in familiar situations at home (adapted with permission from Jill Meciej & Jerry O'Shea, personal communication, 2008).

Key Understanding:
Having clear criteria helps us make good choices.

Materials:
A collection of three pictures for each of the following categories: restaurants, sports, clothes to wear, family fun activities, games to play, TV shows, or other situations in which students have had experiences making choices.

Process:
1. Assign one category to each small group. Tell students they are going to make a list of criteria for deciding which is the best choice in their category. Model doing this with a category you haven't assigned. Then ask each group to make a list of three to five criteria for deciding what the best of their given category would be for their group. If possible, one student in each group records the list for the group. If necessary, circulate and assist with the writing.

2. Tell students they are going to use their criteria to evaluate choices. Model this with three pictures from the category you used to demonstrate creating criteria in Step 1. Then distribute the pictures for their

category. Ask students to evaluate each picture against the list. Which criteria are present in each picture? Which picture would be the best choice for their small group, according to their criteria list?

3. Have small groups take turns sharing their category, the criteria they developed, and their "best" choice from their given pictures. Ask the class to think about other possible choices that would fit the group's criteria, and choices that would not fit the group's criteria. Encourage students to justify their decisions by referring to the small group's criteria.

Closure:

Say, "People make many decisions every day. When making decisions, it is important to think about how the best choice or decision will be determined. Creating a list of criteria is a good way to help us make decisions about different choices."

Lesson 3: Bridging from Home Examples to School Examples.

In this lesson, students will shift from thinking about criteria for choices in their home environment to thinking about criteria in the school environment, beginning with a desired school behavior they are familiar with. In this example, students work in small groups to generate criteria for working in small groups (adapted with permission from Jill Meciej & Jerry O'Shea, personal communication, 2008).

Key Understanding:

Having clear criteria helps us make good decisions about what to do in school.

Materials:

One T-chart with columns labeled "Looks Like"/"Sounds Like" for each small group, plus one for the whole group.

Process:

1. Say, "You're good at choosing things because you have ideas about what makes them good. Now we're going to use that same kind of thinking on something here at school—working in a small group. We're going to think about what it *looks* like and what it *sounds* like when it's done well."

2. Assign students to small groups of three or four. Have them discuss what a group of students *looks* like when they are working well together.

What would someone see while *watching* that group? You may need to give an example to get their thinking started, or you may want to begin this as a whole-group activity for the first one or two descriptors and then let them continue in their small groups. Ask them to come up with three to five words or phrases describing what working well together looks like and list them on their group's T-chart. If necessary, circulate and assist with the writing.

3. Ask students to discuss with their small group what a group of students *sounds* like when they are working well together. What would someone hear while *listening* to that group? Ask them to come up with three to five words or phrases describing what working well together sounds like and list them on their group's T-chart. If necessary, circulate and assist with the writing.

4. Once all groups have finished their lists, create one class T-chart, titled "Criteria for Working in a Group." Tally any criteria identified by multiple groups. Reinforce the idea that what they have listed are *criteria*—descriptors of quality. Ask students to share which they think are most important and why. Have the class vote on the three to five criteria from each list ("Looks Like"/"Sounds Like") they think should be used to judge effectiveness of groups when working together throughout the school year.

Closure:

Say, "We use criteria in school to know what is expected for behavior and for school work. We will use criteria throughout this year so you know what is expected of you in class and in your work. An important responsibility you have as a student is to be sure you know what the criteria will be for the work you are doing. When you are not sure what is expected you can ask me and I will clarify the criteria."

Extension:

Students can follow this process to create a list of criteria for quality for any number of desired behaviors—walking in the hall, lining up for lunch, getting ready to go home. You can model some good and not-so-good behaviors to help their thinking along. You may want to keep the list open and ask them to add to it after especially successful or problematic experiences. When you are satisfied with the criteria list, tell students they can use this list to know what they are doing well and what they need to improve.

Lesson 4: Introducing Pre-existing Criteria.

In this lesson, students apply their criteria-making skills to an academic learning target that will be measured by a scoring guide or developmental continuum describing stages of proficiency. The learning target used as the example is "Gives a presentation."

Key Understanding:

Knowing the criteria in advance helps us perform better.

Materials:

- Chart paper
- Your own short presentation or speech, prepared in advance

Process:

1. Say, "Today we're going to think about the criteria for giving a presentation. You've all seen people give presentations. What does it sound like when we do it really well?" Put "Criteria for a Good Presentation" (or whatever statement describes your oral presentation learning target) as the title on chart paper. Write down what students say.

2. Say, "I'm going to give a short presentation and then we are going to add to our list of criteria things we didn't think of at first. So, watch me and listen to me and think about what I'm doing well." Give a short presentation, modeling for them the characteristics you will teach, e.g., eye contact, volume, enunciation. Invite them to add to the list.

    In the case of this learning target, you could also give a short presentation modeling the not-so-good, such as turning your back to the audience, holding book up in front of your face, and mumbling. (By doing this, you are acting as a "just beginning" oral presentation giver. Be sure you introduce this in such a way that no child will think you are making fun of him or her.) Ask, "What did I do that time?" Let them respond. Then ask, "What could I have done instead to make it better?" Add responses to the list.

3. When your students have come up with a list that has at least some of the criteria you want them to know, tell them, "This is a good list. You have said some of the same things that experts say. Would you like to see the experts' list?" Share the "expert" list—a list of the criteria represented in your scoring guide that you will be teaching them to master. The "expert" list can use terms they either already understand or will learn to understand.

4.   As you present each criterion, ask students if it is similar to anything on their list. Mark the similarities. (Any extraneous ideas they may have come up with can offer you information about misconceptions to address as you help them develop oral presentation skills.) When you finish, be sure to show them how much they already know by reviewing the similarities between their list and the "expert" list.

Closure:

Hand out a rubric or checklist that is suited to your students' reading and comprehension levels. Tell them that you all will be using this "expert" list of criteria to help them practice and become experts at giving presentations.

Prerequisite: A Suitable Rubric

> Explicit scoring criteria, or qualitative descriptors, are essential for giving feedback to students and for engaging students in self-assessment. (Shepard, 2001, p. 1089)

Not all scoring rubrics offer the guidance that students need to improve. The kind of rubric you use is instrumental in determining its usefulness as an instructional tool. If a rubric is to provide feedback to improve student performance, it needs to describe the important elements of quality that students are to pay attention to and strive for.

Rubrics that work best as teaching tools are general, rather than task specific. For example, one of the hallmarks of good writing is the quality of the introduction. A *general* rubric for writing describes the characteristics of a good introduction in such a way that they will apply to any introduction. (See the "Six-trait Analytical Writing Scoring Guide" in Appendix A.) Different writing rubrics may define those characteristics in a slightly different way for different modes (e.g., narrative, expository, persuasive), but you should be able to use the description to judge quality for all writing in that mode. A *task-specific* rubric specifies what a good introduction looks like for this writing assignment only. It includes references to one specific assignment and so cannot be used to evaluate the quality of an introduction for any other assignment. One of the reasons for using general over task-specific rubrics is that you want students to internalize the character-

Nature of the Rubric

The nature of your rubric will determine its usefulness as a teaching tool with students. Not every rubric is suited to this use.

38

istics of quality that apply to all of their work on that particular learning target. Another is that a task-specific rubric gives away "the answer": if handed out in advance, it does all of the thinking for the student and reduces the learning to the level of rote direction following.

To be used as an assessment *for* learning tool, a rubric must be diagnostic—it must describe strengths and weaknesses. Rubrics that use descriptive, rather than evaluative or quantitative, language generally do a far better job of creating a diagnostic picture of quality. For example, one part of a rubric for a science report may relate to display of information. Let us say the rubric has four levels of quality:

Example 1 illustrates descriptive language:

4: Display of information is accurate, complete, and organized so that it is easy to interpret.

3: Display of information is accurate, mostly complete, and is mostly organized so that it is easy to interpret. It may have one or two small omissions.

2: Display of information is partially accurate, partially complete, and may have some organization problems.

1: Display of information is inaccurate, incomplete, and not well organized.

Example 2 illustrates evaluative language:

4: Excellent display of information

3: Good display of information

2: Fair display of information

1: Poor display of information

Example 3 illustrates quantitative language:

4: Displays four pieces of information

3: Displays three pieces of information

2: Displays two pieces of information

1: Displays one piece of information

With descriptive language, students can see what they are doing right as well as what needs work. When the rubric uses only evaluative terms to differentiate the levels, it offers no insight into why something is good or not. And, when we use number counts, as in the third example, unless it is truly the number of instances that determines level of quality, the rubric diagnoses the wrong thing, so it provides inaccurate information.

Another feature to look for is an analytic, rather than holistic structure for complex or multidimensional learning targets. Giving an effective oral presentation, for example, has several components: the content of the speech, its organization, the speaker's delivery, and the speaker's use of language.

Figure 2.10 summarizes the characteristics of scoring rubrics that function well as assessment *for* learning tools. See Appendix A for examples of such rubrics. For more information on types of rubrics and rubric quality, see Arter and Chappuis, 2006; and the DVD, *Developing Performance Assessments for Learning* (Portland, OR: ETS Assessment Training Institute, 2006). See also Stiggins, et al., 2004, Chapter 7.

Figure 2.10

Rubrics as Assessment *for* Learning Tools

This	Not This
General—can be used to judge quality across similar tasks. You can use the same one for different assignments.	**Task specific**—can only be used on one task. You need a different one for each assignment.
Descriptive—includes language that explains characteristics of work or performance at increasing levels of quality	**Evaluative**—uses language that repeats the judgment of the particular score point **Quantitative**—uses languages that counts or measures number of instances

Source: Adapted with permission from J. Arter and J. Chappuis, *Creating and Recognizing Quality Rubrics*, (Portland, OR: ETS Assessment Training Institute, 2006), p. 10.

When to Share the Learning Target

When to communicate learning goals can vary. Sometimes you'll do it as a part of the anticipatory set for the lesson or unit (or whatever content "chunk" you are teaching in): "Today we're going to learn how to write a hypothesis." Other times, such as when a rubric captures the elements of quality, you will want to let the definition unfold over several days or weeks.

Or, you may have created an activity that causes the learning target to reveal itself during the course of the lesson, such as when students engage in discovery learning—a series of explorations structured to develop understanding of the intended learning. In this case, you may not want to post the target in advance. Just make sure they can describe the intended learning *before* you ask them to engage in sustained independent practice and *before* the summative assessment.

However you structure it, make sure that at the appropriate time during the learning, students know what they are aiming for: "We are learning to _____ "; or "I am practicing being able to _____ ." And before students engage in a summative assessment—when you will ask them to show what they have learned—they definitely need to be able to articulate the intended learning: "In this assessment, I am demonstrating my understanding of/ability to/proficiency with _____ ."

Checking for Understanding of the Intended Learning

Periodically, check to see that students can articulate learning goals. You might walk around the room while they are engaged in a task and ask, "Why are we doing this activity?" If you hear responses such as, "to get a grade," "to do all of the problems," "so we can get out early," or other task-completion goals (a.k.a. *performance goals*) instead of "to get better at choosing words that paint a picture in the reader's mind," or "to learn the differences between physical and chemical changes," redirect them with the question, "What are we learning?" If they can't answer it, the learning targets may not be clear enough to them yet. (It's also possible they were under the table looking for a pencil the whole time you were helping them understand the target.)

A more formal window into students' understanding of learning goals is the "exit slip," a short note students use as their ticket out the door at the end of the lesson or period. The idea has been around a long time as one way to achieve closure. To focus exit slips on learning goals, you can ask students to write down what they think you wanted them to learn in the lesson (Harlen, 2007), or respond to the question, "Why did we do _____ (activity) today?"

Another idea is to begin the lesson by phrasing the learning target as a question that students should be able to answer at the end of the lesson. ("How do you find the lowest common denominator for a pair of fractions?" "What is the Pythagorean Theorem and what is it good for?") Have students write a response to the question on an exit slip before they leave (Wiliam & Lee, 2001). You can then read through the exit slips to identify misconceptions and fine tune your plans for the next lesson.

Strategy 2: Use examples and models of strong and weak work.

Strategy 2 strengthens students' evaluative thinking by letting them practice making judgments about accuracy or level of quality with carefully chosen assessment items and examples. The goal here is to help students come to hold an understanding about accuracy and quality similar to yours. This strategy has several different possible applications, depending on the kind of learning target you are teaching and assessment method you will use.

"The features of excellent work should be so transparent that students can learn to evaluate their own work in the same way that their teachers would."

Frederiksen & Collins, 1989, quoted in Shepard, 2001, p. 1092

Knowledge and Reasoning Learning Targets: Selected Response Items

For many knowledge and some reasoning learning targets, the selected response method of assessment serves well formatively (for diagnosis and practice) and summatively (for assigning a mark or grade). This includes multiple-choice, fill-in-the-blank, true/false, and matching items. In general, these kinds of items have one right or best answer (or a small number of acceptable answers) and one or more wrong answers.

A simple way to use selected response items as strong and weak examples is to have students work in pairs to identify an answer they know to be wrong and then explain why it is wrong. They can do the same thing for the right answer, but they generally have more fun with the wrong answers and they learn just as much, if not more, trying to figure out what the problem with an answer is. (You will find more in-depth teaching ideas with selected response items in Chapter 5.)

Reasoning, Performance Skill, and Product Learning Targets: Performance Assessment Methodology

Students not only need to understand the language of the rubric (Strategy 1), but they also need to be able to differentiate between a performance or product done well and one with problems. This prepares them to understand your feedback to them and to engage in peer- and self-assessment.

"'That's a 5. I don't know what it means. I've got it on some of my work. I think it's a grade thing.'"

Harlen, 2007, p. 126

Selecting Samples

To implement Strategy 2 with a performance assessment, you can use samples of student work to familiarize them with the levels of quality described by your rubric. Begin by finding (or creating) anonymous samples of strong work as well as work that exhibits one or more problems that you want students to begin noticing and correcting in their own work. Use only examples from students *not* in the class that will be using them and keep them anonymous (Figure 2.11).

 Anonymity

When providing examples for students to practice evaluating, use only anonymous work not done by anyone in the class. Letting students practice evaluating work with the student present, even if no one knows whose work it is, is risky. You are better off not taking the chance of risking harm to any of your students.

Keep in mind that this is not yet an exercise in offering peer feedback; rather, it is practice for being able to do that well.

Figure 2.11

Gathering Anonymous Samples

- Find annotated samples on state or provincial websites.

- Ask students for permission to use their work as a teaching example and then save it for next year, trade with another teacher, or use it with a different class. (Students own their work, so be sure to ask for permission before you use it or trade it.)

- Create your own examples, inserting the kind of errors students typically make.

A Protocol for Using Anonymous Samples with Students

For this activity students will use the scoring rubric to evaluate the anonymous samples you have collected. Begin by selecting one trait (criterion) from the scoring guide to focus on. In choosing a trait to start with, consider what students will need to know first. For example, using the Mathematics Problem-solving rubric, you may decide to focus on the trait of *Problem Solving* before moving to the trait of *Mathematical Communication*, because if they don't first learn how to choose an appropriate strategy and work it through to completion, they won't have much to communicate about.

Next, select one or more samples in the strong range, the weak range, and the midrange for the trait you have decided to begin with. Initially, use samples that have clearly defined strengths and problems. When students have had some practice with them, you can move to the midrange samples. Prepare the samples so that you can show them to the whole class, either for display on a screen or for distribution to each student (overhead transparencies, single copies for the light table/Elmo, paper copies, etc.).

Begin Simply

Keep your examples fairly uncomplicated the first few times, while students are learning the protocol.

Beginning with a strong sample, follow this protocol, which is set up for use with a five-point rubric:

1. Display, show, or distribute the sample. Read it aloud, if appropriate. For performances and some product characteristics, reading aloud either won't be useful or it won't be possible (e.g., not useful: Accurate Display of Data in science; Mathematical Concepts and Procedures; Conventions in writing; not possible: all nonwritten products, such as art products; all performances). In some cases, such as with mathematics problem solving, students will need to carry out the task before viewing samples for evaluation.

2. Ask students to decide independently whether they think the sample is strong or weak for the trait they are focusing on. If they think it is strong, have them begin reading the scoring rubric at the high end. If the words and phrases for the highest level describe it, they can assign it a "5." If they think it may not be quite that strong, have them read the middle level. If the middle level describes it completely, they can assign it a "3." If the sample has some strengths from the high level and some problems from the middle level, then they should mark the phrases they think apply in each level and assign the example a "4." Conversely, if they think it is weak, have them begin reading at the low end. If the

words and phrases from the lowest level describe it, they can assign it a "1." If they think it may not be quite that weak, have them read the middle level. If the middle level describes it completely, they can assign it a "3." If the sample has some weaknesses from the lowest level and some strengths noted at the middle level, then they should mark the phrases they think apply in each level and assign the example a "2."

3. After students have had the opportunity to settle on a score individually, ask them to work in small groups to discuss their judgments and the reasons why, using the language of the scoring rubric. This is very important—the purpose for the activity is to deepen their understanding of the scoring rubric, so as they are discussing, walk around the class reinforcing students' use of the rubric's language and concepts to support their judgments.

4. Next, ask students to vote as a class and tally their choices: How many gave this a "1?" a "2?" a "3?" a "4?" a "5?" Then, ask for volunteers to share what they gave it and why. Listen for use of the rubric language. Do not worry if student opinions differ at first. During this stage of the activity, encourage them to respond to each other. Consider refraining from expressing your opinion at this point; comment only on their use of the concepts in the rubric to justify their scores: "Good job of using the language of the rubric to justify your score." If a student justifies a score with a reason not in the rubric, you might say, "Can you find language in the rubric that supports your score?" or, "You noticed something that is actually described in a different trait. We'll be getting to that later."

5. You can share the score that you (and other raters, if you are using samples that have been rated and annotated by others) would give it, but rather than give a lengthy explanation, you may wish to let them repeat the process with another example, this time a much weaker one, so they can discover and internalize how degrees of quality manifest themselves.

6. Repeat this process until students are familiar with the language and concepts of the scoring rubric. As they get better at differentiating between strong and weak work, begin using midrange samples.

After students have engaged in this activity several times, you can turn more responsibility over to them in small groups. Figure 2.12 shows a table protocol—instructions you can give students, where one student in each group becomes the moderator of the discussion, the role you played while they were learning how to score. If the job of moderator rotates among the group, each person also gets the opportunity to listen for use of the language of the rubric to justify scores.

Figure 2.12

Table Protocol for Analyzing Sample Papers

Students working in small groups can follow this protocol to work through the process of analyzing samples for one or more criteria (traits) on the scoring rubric. They can take turns around the table acting as moderator.

1. Everyone reads the scoring guide for _____ (specify trait) in this order: the highest level, the lowest level, and then the middle level or levels.

2. The moderator reads the sample paper aloud.

3. Everyone else thinks, "Strong or weak for _____ (specified trait)?" while listening to the paper.

4. Everyone (including the moderator) silently and independently reads the high or low level of the rubric corresponding to their own judgments of strong or weak. If the high or low level doesn't describe the sample well, then read the middle level (or levels progressing toward the middle) until you find the phrases that accurately describe the quality of the sample. Everyone writes down their score.

5. When all are ready, the moderator conducts the vote and tallies the scores.

6. The moderator conducts the discussion—"What did you give it and why?"—encouraging the use of the scoring rubric's language and concepts.

Examples of Strategies 1 and 2 with Elementary Students

The following scenario, transcribed from a demonstration teaching lesson, is an example of how you can use a student-friendly version of a reasoning learning target as the basis of a lesson. In this case, the teacher is introducing fourth graders to the reading learning target, "Makes inferences based on what is read." As you read through the scenario, look for Strategy 1, introducing the definition of *inference*, and Strategy 2, using strong and weak examples.

Inference Scenario

TEACHER: "Have any of you ever known what you're getting for a present before you opened the package?" (Hands wave in the air.) "What was it? Luke?"

LUKE: "It was a basketball."

TEACHER: "How did you know it was a basketball? Did it say 'To Luke—Basketball' on the tag?"

LUKE: "Noooo. I knew it was one because I asked for it, and it was round, and it bounced."

TEACHER: "So you made a guess, based on clues."

LUKE: "Yeah."

TEACHER: "How about you, Sarah?"

SARAH: "It was a bike."

TEACHER: "What were your clues?"

SARAH: "Well my mom said it was a pony, but I knew it was a bike."

TEACHER: "How did you know it wasn't a pony?"

SARAH: "It was too skinny."

(The teacher then asks for other examples—"What did you get? How did you know?"—reiterating the concept that students made correct guesses based on clues.)

TEACHER: "You all made guesses and you were right because you had some clues. When we make a guess based on clues, we call that an *inference*." (She writes the word *"inference"* and the definition *"a guess based on clues"* on a piece of chart paper.) "Let's practice inferring some more." (She walks up to a student wearing a turquoise sweater.) "I'm going to make an inference that Maria's favorite color is turquoise. Maria, is your favorite color turquoise?"

MARIA: "Well, no."

TEACHER: "What happened here? I made a guess and I based it on a clue. What went wrong?"

STUDENTS: "You didn't have enough clues." "Just because she's wearing a turquoise sweater today doesn't mean she loves it." "Maria hardly ever wears turquoise."

TEACHER: "What would I have to see in order to make a confident guess that her favorite color is turquoise?"

STUDENTS: "All her pencils would be turquoise." "The mirror in her locker would be turquoise." "She would wear turquoise every day."

TEACHER: "So it's not enough to have one clue to make a good inference. I might need three or four clues."

JAMAL: "Well if she wore turquoise every day, that's just one clue, but it happens over and over."

TEACHER: "So we could call that a repeated clue? An inference, to be a good one, needs to be based on enough clues—more than one piece of evidence or the same evidence repeated over and over?"

JAMAL: "Yeah."

TEACHER: "Let's call this a level 3 inference." (Under the definition of inference, she writes: 3 = *A guess based on enough clues.*) "Now, think about the guess that Maria's favorite color is turquoise. Let's call that a level 2 inference. How would we define that? It's a guess, but what's wrong with it?"

JAMAL: "It doesn't have enough clues."

(The teacher writes 2 = *A guess, but not enough clues.*)

TEACHER: "Okay. Now what if I guessed that Jerome's favorite color is orange. What would you call that? Is it an inference? It's a guess isn't it?" (Jerome is not wearing any orange.)

STUDENTS: "Yeah but you don't have any evidence."

TEACHER: "What kind of an inference is it?"

STUDENTS: "A bad one."

TEACHER: "So, we could call a poor inference a *wild* guess because it's not based on any clues. Let's call this a level 1 inference." (The teacher writes: 1 = *Wild guess—no clues.*)

In this example, the teacher is guiding students in developing a simple scoring rubric for quality inferences by using strong and weak examples to help them get a clear vision of exactly what constitutes a high-quality response to an inference question. Figure 2.13 shows the inference rubric they developed, along with the posters she used to illustrate the definition. Contrast this short lesson with telling students that to *infer* means to "read between the lines." That definition itself requires an inference to understand.

Figure 2.13

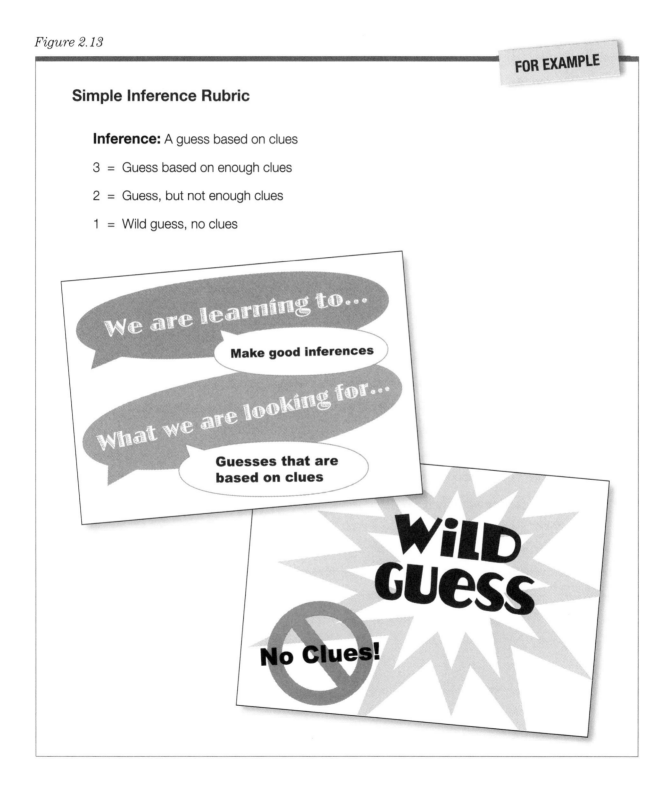

Simple Inference Rubric

Inference: A guess based on clues

3 = Guess based on enough clues

2 = Guess, but not enough clues

1 = Wild guess, no clues

Second grade teacher Amy Meyer used Strategies 1 and 2 to introduce the learning targets for a writing project (Figure 2.14). Here is her description of what she did and what happened with students as a result (personal communication, 2008):

> I introduced each writing target, one by one, in a minilesson. I provided examples and models of each writing piece so students could see what I wanted their work to look like. As a group we looked at strong and weak examples. The students had a clear vision of what they needed to do for their writing project. Using models and the specific targets helped students understand more clearly what I expected. Their work was much better than what they had done in a previous activity without the targets and models.

Figure 2.14

FOR EXAMPLE

How Can I Make a Story Enjoyable to Read?

- I can make a plan for my story that includes a main character, a problem, and a solution.

- I can talk my story out or tell it out loud to a writing partner to work out any "clunks."

- I can write a bold beginning to get the reader hooked.

- I can describe my character in my story. I can tell about appearance (looks) and character traits (personality) in my story.

- I can write a story that has a clear beginning, middle, and end.

- I can describe the problem the character has and how the character solves that problem using supporting details.

- I can use juicy words and "showing" sentences to make my story entertaining to the reader.

Source: Used with permission from Amy Meyer, unpublished classroom materials, Olentangy Local School District, Lewis Center, OH, 2008.

Conclusion

By making the learning targets or goals clear to students from the outset, we build student confidence and increase the chances that students will reach the target. With Strategy 1, we provide students with descriptive statements in language they can understand. With Strategy 2, we offer examples to illustrate levels of quality. Both are necessary for students to internalize a vision of where they're headed. If you had to choose one thing to do from all the recommendations in this book, it would be most profitable to start with an activity in this chapter.

CHAPTER 3

Where Am I Now?
Effective Feedback

Strategy 3
Offer regular descriptive feedback.

Strategy 3
Offer regular descriptive feedback.

Formative assessment *does* make a difference, and it is the quality, not just the quantity, of feedback that merits our closest attention. By quality of feedback, we now realise we have to understand not just the technical structure of the feedback (such as its accuracy, comprehensiveness and appropriateness) but also its accessibility to the learner (as a communication), its catalytic and coaching value, and its ability to inspire confidence and hope.

—*Sadler, 1998, p. 84 [emphasis in original]*

W hen learning to play a sport, student athletes practice regularly, with feedback, before they are expected to play in the game that counts toward the team record. Coaches don't teach their sport by scheduling twenty games and then pulling players out during the game to introduce the fundamentals. They schedule practices to get in as much time with their players as possible before the first game of the season. And once practices begin, players don't just run through mock competitions. Coaches teach the fundamentals of the sport through explanation and demonstration, and offer feedback during practice on what players are doing right and what they need to change.

Effective feedback in the classroom operates much the same way: its role is to help students identify where they are now with respect to where they are headed, and to prompt further learning. Yet teachers and coaches alike know from experience that what works with one student may not work with another. Sometimes feedback doesn't have the effect we had hoped it would, because students don't always act on it. The type and timing of feedback can dramatically alter its effectiveness. Explaining the research on feedback, Shepard (2008) states,

> Surprisingly, however, feedback is not always or even usually successful. Kluger and De Nisi's (1996) meta-analysis cautions that in one third of studies feedback worsens performance, when evaluation focuses on the person rather than the task. In one third of comparisons there is no difference in outcomes with and without feedback. Only in the one third of studies where the feedback focused on substantive elements of the task, giving specific guidance on how to improve, did feedback consistently improve performance. (pp. 284–285)

Providing feedback can be a labor-intensive proposition. If we put all that time in we want to make sure that (1) we're doing it right, and (2) students will use it. In other words, we want to maximize the chances that student achievement will improve as a result. In the first part of this chapter we'll examine characteristics of feedback that make it more or less effective in influencing learning in the classroom. In the second part, we'll delve into strategies for offering feedback, streamlining the process, and teaching students to give feedback to each other.

Characteristics of Effective Feedback

The *presence* of feedback does not improve learning. It is its *quality* that determines its effectiveness. So what is the best kind of feedback to give? As Shepard (2008) notes, researchers' conclusions are complex. However, several commonalities do emerge. Effective feedback has the following characteristics: (1) it directs attention to the intended learning, pointing out strengths and offering specific information to guide improvement; (2) it occurs during learning, while there is still time to act on it; (3) it addresses partial understanding; (4) it does not do the thinking for the student; and (5) it limits corrective information to the amount of advice the student can act on (Figure 3.1).

"Feedback is effective when it consists of information about progress, and/or about how to proceed."

Hattie & Timperley, 2007, p. 89

In a nutshell, effective feedback acts like a global positioning system for students, telling them how close they are to the target and what steps they can take to reach it.

Figure 3.1

> **Characteristics of Effective Feedback**
>
> 1. Directs attention to the intended learning, pointing out strengths and offering specific information to guide improvement
>
> 2. Occurs during learning, while there is still time to act on it
>
> 3. Addresses partial understanding
>
> 4. Does not do the thinking for the student
>
> 5. Limits corrective information to the amount of advice the student can act on

1. Effective feedback directs attention to the intended learning.

Feedback that directs attention to the intended learning does so by focusing on characteristics of the work the student has done or on characteristics of the process used. It points out what the student has done well (*success* feedback), and gives specific information to guide improvement (*intervention* feedback).

Success Feedback

All students need to know when they are doing something well or right. Even finding relative success ("the strongest part of your solution is . . .") will work as long as it's genuine and specifically linked to the intended learning. This is particularly helpful for lower-achieving students or for any students who are in early stages of developing proficiency. Success feedback identifies what was done correctly, describes a feature of quality that is present in the work, or points out effective use of a strategy or process. For example:

- "You got all of the questions on parallel and perpendicular lines right."

- "The information you found is important to your topic and answers questions the reader is likely to have."

- "The table you drew really helped solve the problem."

- "I see that while you were revising you noticed you needed to gather more information about censorship cases before going on. I think that will improve your argument."

- "You have made your pencil marks so they line up exactly with the marks on the ruler."

Intervention Feedback

Intervention feedback identifies areas in need of improvement and provides enough information so that the student understands what to do next. It, too, is most effective when linked to the intended learning goals. Intervention feedback can do one or more of the following: identify a correction, describe a specific feature of quality that needs work, or point out an ineffective or incorrect use of strategy or process. In addition, it points the way to further action by offering a reminder, making a specific suggestion, or asking a question that opens up a course of action for the student. For example:

- "You had some trouble with the differences between isosceles and scalene triangles. Reread page 102 and try these again."

- "Remember what we have learned about converting mixed numbers to improper fractions. Try using that process before subtracting."

- "The meaning of the paraphrased information in paragraph 3 does not come through clearly enough yet. Try underlining the key ideas in the original and then rewriting them in your own words. Then try the paragraph again."

- "The drawing you made didn't seem to help you solve the problem. Try drawing a Venn diagram and placing the information in it."

- "Try putting your arguments into the graphic organizer for persuasive writing and look for holes."

- "You have to make your pencil marks so they line up exactly with the marks on the ruler, or the lines you draw won't be parallel."

- "This ruler is too short to draw the lines you need. Try using a 12-inch ruler."

Notice that in the previous examples, students are given information that prompts an action. We don't always need to offer the whole solution, however. Often, we can help students think about what to do by asking a question:

- "The meaning of the paraphrased information in paragraph 3 does not come through clearly enough yet. What might you do to make it clearer?"

- "The drawing you made didn't seem to help you solve the problem. What other kind of drawing might work?"

If intervention feedback isn't clear to students, it can cause a whole host of problems. In their synthesis of research on effective feedback, Hattie and Timperley (2007) summarize the dangers:

> There can be deleterious effects on feelings of self-efficacy and performance when students are unable to relate the feedback to the cause of their poor performance. Unclear evaluative feedback, which fails to clearly specify the grounds on which students have met with achievement success or otherwise, is likely to exacerbate negative outcomes, engender uncertain self-images, and lead to poor performance. (p. 95)

Figure 3.2

Success and Intervention Feedback Options

Success Feedback Options	<ul><li>Identify what is done correctly.</li><li>Describe a feature of quality present in the work.</li><li>Point out effective use of strategy or process.</li></ul>
Intervention Feedback Options	<ul><li>Identify a correction.</li><li>Describe a feature of quality needing work.</li><li>Point out a problem with strategy or process.</li><li>Offer a reminder.</li><li>Make a specific suggestion.</li><li>Ask a question.</li></ul>

What is missing from these attempts at corrective feedback?

- Try these again

- Incomplete

- Keep studying

- More effort needed

Nobody wakes up in the morning and says, "Today I think I'll harm students," but if students don't understand our feedback or know how to act on it, it can undermine their sense of *self-efficacy*—their belief that effort can lead to success. The key question is, "Can *this* student take action on the basis of *this* comment?"

Figure 3.3 gives more examples of success and intervention feedback. The comments link directly to learning targets. They relate either to the work the student has produced or the process used, pointing out strengths and offering specific guidance for next steps. Notice the kinds of interventions in each: reminders, suggestions, and/or corrections. When you hear that feedback needs to be specific, this is what that means.

For primary students, success and intervention feedback can take the form of "That's good!" and "That's next!" For example: "I see you have . . ." (that's good). "Now let's see you . . ." (that's next). See Figure 3.4 for samples of feedback with younger students.

Establishing a Forward-looking Stance Toward Learning

By using the terms *success* and *intervention* to describe kinds of feedback, we can steer students away from interpreting feedback as "positive" or "negative." Success feedback is indeed positive, but intervention feedback is not necessarily negative. For example, you may notice that a student is using a comma to separate two complete thoughts in a sentence. Your intervention feedback can be, "You're ready for semicolons," which is a forward-looking stance toward a mistake. The role of intervention feedback is to offer information—a reminder, a suggestion, or a correction—or to pose a question, so that further effort will bring the student closer to successful achievement, in such a way that the student is not discouraged from trying again.

With that in mind, not every feedback comment must include reference to a strength to be effective. Neither does all feedback need to include both success

Figure 3.3

Success and Intervention Feedback Comments

Social Studies:

Let's say your content standard is "Understands ways in which native and immigrant cultures have contributed to form American culture," and you have translated that into a series of "I can" statements, one of which is "I can describe similarities and differences between people in the English settlements and those in the French and Spanish settlements." When students do an assignment that addresses this target, the assignment itself might specify that you are looking for accurate information about each culture, important details about each culture, and accurate categorization of information into similarities and differences.

Feedback emphasizing these learning goals then relates to one or more of the features you asked students to include: "All of the information you gave about the English settlements is accurate." Or "Please recheck your facts. Some of the information you gave about English settlements is not true for all English settlements." (Suggestion + correction)

Science:

Let's say the content standard you are teaching to is "Understands how to plan and conduct scientific investigations," and as a part of making that content standard clear, you have introduced a rubric for scientific inquiry that includes creating a good hypothesis as a component. Specifically, it states that a strong hypothesis includes a prediction with a cause-effect reason.

Feedback emphasizing the learning goal can use that language: "What you have written is a hypothesis because it is a prediction about what will happen. You can improve it by giving a reason explaining why you think that will happen." (Success + suggestion)

Mathematics:

Let's say your content standard is "Uses a problem-solving strategy to construct a solution," and you have introduced a scoring rubric that includes Mathematical Problem Solving as one of its traits.

You can use that language to offer feedback: "Your strategy worked for part of the problem, but it didn't lead to a correct solution because it fell apart right here. What other strategy could you use to deal with this remaining group of people?" (Success + correction + suggestion elicited from the student)

Figure 3.4

FOR EXAMPLE

Success and Intervention Feedback with Younger Students

How might this work with younger students? It can be as simple as pointing out which of their letter "J"s matches the standard: "This is a good letter 'J.' Do you know what makes it a good one?" Or you can identify which is their best one and then give a pointer for making it better: "This is a good 'J' because you have the hook going in the right direction. For your next 'J,' see if you can get it to sit on the line."

Or, let's say you are teaching students to use details in their writing. For the first-grader who wrote "The Tent," (see accompanying figure) feedback emphasizing the learning goal may sound like this: "Look at those details! I can tell you've examined how zippers work because you have drawn all the teeth at an angle. Good writers notice details others might overlook, just like you did." Contrast this descriptive feedback with feedback that praises the work without giving any specific information: "Wow! What a great story!"

Or, if you'd like to describe a success and offer an intervention: "We've been reading stories that have a beginning, a middle, and an end. I see you've included a beginning and a middle in your story, just like good writers do. Next, see if you can write (or draw) the end." The feedback refers to the learning goals, in this case by using the language of quality ("We've been reading stories that have a beginning, a middle, and an end"); it shows the student what she has done well ("You've included a beginning and a middle in your story, just like good writers do"); and it offers a suggestion for the next step, also related to the learning goals ("Next, see if you can write [or draw] the end").

and intervention remarks. Your comments needn't come across as artificial or formulaic; you will want to use your own judgment, taking into account what *this* student needs at *this* point in his learning.

Additionally, there is no universal caveat that feedback must be limited to commenting only on the specific learning target of the lesson. If students' work is in response to a practice lesson, it is most often a good idea to stick to the focus of the lesson in your comments, so students can take full advantage of the opportunity to improve. (See Chapter 5 for further explanation of focused lessons.) However, sometimes you will offer feedback beyond the focus of a certain lesson, in which case it can be appropriate to give success or corrective comments relating to concepts or skills previously taught, as when students are in the process of preparing a final performance or product. Here again, it is a matter of your professional judgment. Just be careful that the feedback does not focus on trivia unrelated to the learning targets.

Praise as Success Feedback

Although many students enjoy praise, if the praise is directed to characteristics of the *learner* rather than to characteristics of the *work* or the *process used*, it appears to be less effective both as a motivator and as an agent for improved achievement. In general, praise as a motivator is unpredictable and often counterproductive. Praise can have a negative effect on learning because it directs students' attention away from the learning and onto what the teacher thinks of them: "The teacher thinks I'm smart/not smart." "The teacher likes me/doesn't like me." In meta-analyses of studies comparing the two types of feedback, work-related feedback in all cases was far more powerful in effecting change in achievement (Ames, 1992; Black & Wiliam, 1998a; Hattie & Timperley, 2007; Shepard, 2008). Too often, praise does not provide information of value either to reinforce the learning or take action to change it. In addition, students' responses to praise vary widely, influenced by past experiences and self-concepts. Work-related feedback does a much better job of developing students' belief that effort will lead to success.

Praise for intelligence can even have some surprisingly negative results. In a study examining the effects of praise for effort or intelligence on learners' persistence and achievement, Blackwell, Trzesniewski, and Dweck (2007) found that recognizing effort ("Look how hard you tried!"), which students see as a variable within their control, is much more beneficial than praising intelligence ("Look how smart you are!"), which students tend to see as personal attribute they cannot change. (Figure 3.5 presents a summary of the Blackwell et al. [2007] study.) Dweck (2007) explains,

> [For students with a fixed mindset,] mistakes crack their self-confidence because they attribute errors to lack of ability, which they feel powerless to change. They avoid challenges because challenges make mistakes more likely and looking smart less so. [They] shun effort in the belief that having to work hard means they are dumb. [Students with a growth mindset] think intelligence is malleable and can be developed through education and hard work. They want to learn above all else. After all, if you believe that you can expand your intellectual skills, you want to do just that. Because slipups stem from a lack of effort, not ability, they can be remedied by more effort. Challenges are energizing, rather than intimidating; they offer opportunities to learn. (p. 2)

"Enhancing student motivation, however, is not about enhancing self-concept of ability. . . . Enhancing motivation means enhancing children's valuing of effort and a commitment to effort-based strategies . . . "

Ames, 1992, p. 268

Is school about learning or is it about competition for grades and recognition? How we talk to students about their successes shapes how they see the goal of school and how they will respond in the face of challenge, either with resiliency or with fear-based failure-avoidance behaviors.

Praise and Intrinsic Motivation

A student's level of effort may be driven by an internal desire to achieve, and not the desire to get a reward, such as praise or a high grade. We want to be careful that we don't reduce a student's intrinsic motivation—the desire to do something for its own sake, or because of an internal drive—by assuming that an extrinsic motivator—reward or praise—will reinforce it. Extrinsic motivation can reduce students' desire to do something they initially had intrinsic motivation to do. We can make students dependent on rewards, which can harm learning, even though our intention is to help it.

Recognition for effort can direct students' attention back to their work, by helping them make the link between what they tried and where they experienced success as a result: "This time is better than last time because you. . . ." When students' efforts don't produce success, use feedback that offers "direction correction" to maximize the chances that further effort will produce satisfactory results. In this situation, you may be able to offer a thought ("Consider this . . ."), a suggestion for further learning ("Read this . . ."), or information ("Add this . . .").

Effort feedback should be genuine—it is important to keep in mind that the student is the only person who truly knows how much effort went into any task. You may want to acknowledge effort with a statement such as, "It looks to me like you put a great deal of effort into this. Tell me what you did."

"I like the way you . . ."

Many of us were taught to begin feedback statements with the phrase, "I like the way you . . ." , which may imply that pleasing the teacher is the key to quality. If your students repeatedly ask, "Is this what you want?", it's possible they have internalized "quality = pleasing the teacher." Sure, quality pleases us, but the best use of our feedback is to help students internalize the *aspects of quality* that make their work good. Prefacing task-related remarks with a praise statement reduces the effectiveness of the information that follows—students are less likely to remember it.

Comments emphasizing learning goals have been repeatedly shown to lead to greater learning gains than comments emphasizing self-esteem.

Ames, 1992; Butler, 1988; Hattie & Timperley, 2007

As you think about your own practices in the classroom, be careful about using praise in a way that labels the student, such as, "You are excellent." If honest expressions of praise are a natural part of your dialogue with students, direct praise statements to the work the student has produced and include features of the work that make it praiseworthy: "Your math solution is excellent because..."

Grades as Feedback on Practice Work

One of the problems of expecting marks or grades to act as feedback on practice work is that they do not communicate details about what students understand or don't understand. Grades are not really feedback; they are summary evaluative judgments about the level of achievement. They don't describe the quality of the work. Does a "C" alone tell a student what she has done well? Does it show her which parts of the learning she still needs to work on?

It might be tempting to think that offering comments along with grades on practice work will solve the problem. A number of studies have shown, however, that attaching evaluative grades to practice work can cause problems for both high- and low-achieving students (Black & Wiliam, 1998a). In one interesting and often-cited study, Butler (1988) found that assigning grades to practice work inhibited further learning and that students ignored comments when they were accompanied by grades. Your own experience may confirm that many students pay more attention to the evaluative mark/grade than to the comments,

Figure 3.5

RESEARCH SNAPSHOT

"Implicit Theories of Intelligence Predict
Achievement Across an Adolescent Transition:
A Longitudinal Study and an Intervention"

Blackwell, Trzesniewski, & Dweck, 2007

Hypothesis:

Adolescents who believe intelligence is malleable (can be developed through
education and hard work) will demonstrate persistence in the face of setbacks
and will outperform those who believe intelligence is a fixed trait (you are
born with a certain amount).

Who Was Involved:

Students entering seventh grade each year for four years (for a total of 373
students), followed over the course of their seventh- and eighth-grade years
in an urban junior high school. Students were described as "moderately high
achieving."

What They Did:

At the beginning of their seventh-grade year, students were identified as
having either an *incremental theory of intelligence* (growth mindset)
or an *entity theory of intelligence* (fixed mindset) by responding to a
questionnaire with statements such as "Your intelligence is something very
basic about you that you can't really change" and others regarding their beliefs
about whether intelligence is something they can change or not. They also
answered questions designed to measure their learning goals, effort beliefs,
and response to failure (failure attribution and subsequent strategy selection).

Students' baseline achievement in mathematics was determined by a
standardized mathematics achievement test taken in the spring of their sixth-
grade year. Seventh-grade fall and spring term grades and eighth-grade fall

and spring term grades served to measure achievement during the study. (All students in the study within the same grade had the same curriculum and the same teacher.)

What the Researchers Found:

At the outset of the study, "growth mindset" and "fixed mindset" students' achievement scores in mathematics were comparable. At the end of the first semester, the growth mindset students' mathematics grades were higher than those of the fixed mindset students. The gap between the two groups' mathematics grades widened over the two years. Students with a growth mindset also were found to hold more positive motivational beliefs than did students with the fixed mindset. Characteristics of a growth mindset included valuing learning over getting good grades; believing that the more you work at something the better you can become; and in the face of a setback, such as a disappointing grade, studying harder or attempting a different strategy. Characteristics of a fixed mindset included valuing looking smart over learning; believing that if you have to work hard, it means you have low ability; and in the face of a setback, such as a disappointing grade, studying less, avoiding taking the subject again, and considering cheating on subsequent tasks.

Source: Summarized from L. Blackwell, K. Trzesniewski, & C. Dweck, Implicit theories of intelligence predict achievement across an adolescent transition: A longitudinal study and an intervention. *Child Development 78*(1), 2007, pp. 246–263.

even on practice work. When the purpose of the assignment is formative—to help students improve—it can be counterproductive to include a summative mark/grade along with the feedback.

Consider not putting evaluative marks/grades on practice work until the feedback has been acted on. Or, write the evaluative mark/grade in pencil, their "would-be" grade. Tell students they can erase it by acting on the feedback—this is the grade that you currently have in your record book, and it is the grade they would receive if they stopped here, but they're not finished yet, so it's not their final grade. Then write the final evaluative mark in pen on the finished work. (You can also use the "pencil/pen" system for keeping formative and summative marks separate in your record book.)

2. Effective feedback occurs during learning.

My first year of teaching I set out to post a sign that said, "It's okay to make mistakes in this room." When I copied it out on a sentence strip, I ran out of room for the word "room." I wrote it two more times, each time getting only one more letter squeezed in. I hung the third version, with the last letters running up the side, because it showed what it told (Figure 3.6).

Even though we say to students, "We learn from our mistakes," very few of them view an error as their friend. In the words of a panicked high school freshman, "In that class *all* of my mistakes count against me. I'm doomed." How do we *show* students that it's not only okay to make mistakes, but that when they occur, they are to be welcomed as information about next steps in learning?

"If assessment insights are to be used to move learning along rather than merely tally how much learning has occurred so far, then assessment has to occur in the middle of instruction, not just at the end points . . ."

Shepard, 2001, p. 1086

We cultivate this mindset when we offer feedback with opportunities to improve *during* the learning. Feedback is most effective in improving achievement if it is delivered while there is still time to act on it, which means *before* the graded event. If practice work counts toward the mark or grade, mistakes do count against the student. When students take a quiz, for example, the score does not have to be used for marking/grading purposes; rather it can serve you and the students as information about what they understand and what they need to improve. You, and they, can record the score, but including it as evidence of final achievement penalizes those students who have not

Figure 3.6

> # It's okay to make mistakes in this room

yet reached mastery. If you want the results to increase learning, students are better served by looking at the quiz and asking, "What does this tell me I know? What do I still need to work on?" (In Chapter 4 you will find examples of how tests and quizzes can be set up so students can use them to self-assess and set goals for further learning.)

Feedback can encourage students to see mistakes as leading to further learning if you plan time for students to take the actions suggested, before asking them to demonstrate their level of achievement for a mark or grade. The time we spend giving feedback may be wasted if we do not build in time for them to act on it. The question here is, "Where is the practice?" The answer points us to the optimum venue for feedback.

Other Feedback Variables to Consider

Providing information related to the intended learning by describing strengths and areas for improvement and offering time to act on the information are the primary requirements of effective feedback. However, three additional characteristics also influence feedback's ability to generate greater achievement:

- It addresses partial understanding.
- It does not do the thinking for the student.
- It limits corrective information to the amount of advice the student can act on.

3. Effective feedback addresses partial understanding.

Offering feedback is not always the appropriate instructional intervention to use. It is most effective when it addresses faulty understanding, rather than a total lack of understanding. For example, think about this comment:

> *"Remember, a generalization is a statement that's accurate for the evidence at hand and also applies to broader array of instances. Your generalization doesn't take into account the characteristics of all meat-eating plants. How do you think you will need to change it?"*

A student who is lost in the content is not likely to understand the direction given in this corrective feedback; it can even cause him to feel worse because he has failed twice: "I don't know how to do this and I don't understand what you're telling me to do about it."

Look at the two samples of student mathematics solutions in Figure 3.7. Both students attempted to use the strategy of drawing a picture: one drew a canteen and the other drew stick figures. Which one shows partial mastery? Which one is struggling with the basics? Which one would benefit from feedback? Which one probably needs further instruction to move ahead?

If the work indicates that students have not yet attained partial mastery of the concepts—if, for example, there is nothing you can offer success feedback on—continued teaching is apt to be far more efficient than attempting to initiate learning through comments. Also, if you find yourself offering the same feedback repeatedly to large numbers of students, perhaps it's time for a one-size-fits-all review lesson. This saves you time in the long run and eliminates the risk that offering insightful feedback has been replaced by nagging. When students do not yet have the knowledge base they need to act on intervention feedback, teaching suggestions from Strategies 5 and 6 (found in Chapter 5) may help move students from "just beginning" to "part-way there" and so prepare them to participate in the self-monitoring cycle that feedback introduces.

> "Corrective feedback can be ignored by students if it is poorly presented or if the student's knowledge is insufficient to accommodate additional feedback information."
>
> *Hattie & Timperley, 2007, p. 100*

Figure 3.7

FOR EXAMPLE

Student Mathematics Solution

Problem: A group of eight people are all going camping for three days and need to carry their own water. They read in a guide book that 12.5 liters are needed for a party of 5 people for 1 day. Based on the guide book, what is the minimum amount of water the 8 people should carry all together? Explain your answer.

Sample 1

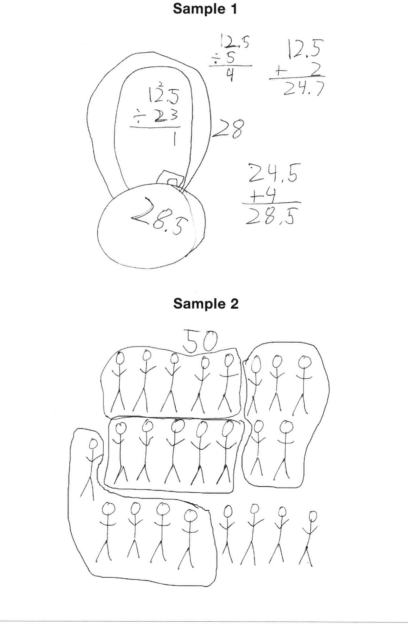

Sample 2

Source: Adapted with permission from R. Stiggins, J. Arter, J. Chappuis, and S. Chappuis, *Classroom Assessment* for *Student Learning: Doing It Right—Using It Well*: Activities & Resources CD-ROM (Portland, OR: ETS Assessment Training Institute, 2004), Chapter 7, "Student Math Problem Solving."

4. Effective feedback does not do the thinking for the student.

In some cases, intervention feedback may eliminate the cognitive challenge of a task so that the student is no longer required to think at all—her only "next step" is to follow the directions provided in the feedback. When this happens, we may have offered too much help.

Imagine saying to a child at home, "Please clean up your room." And then, "Clean up your room, please." And then, "Clean up your room, *now*." And finally going in and doing it for her. We usually don't clean the room ourselves for a very good reason: if we do, we'll train her to wait us out.

How does this relate to feedback? Do we ever remind students of what to correct and then when they do an incomplete job, we take over and finish the work for them? In my early teaching years, I did this with student writing. I would ask students to edit their papers for spelling, capitalization, and punctuation. They would turn in papers with some of the errors fixed and then I would fix the mistakes they didn't catch. I was "over-feedbacking"—instead of pointing the way to success, I was doing their work for them. This is a lot like me cleaning my teenager's bedroom at home. The more I do, the less she will do, which I know from experience.

What are the alternatives? In the bedroom instance, I first check to see that she knows how to clean it. Then we work on her ability to notice what needs doing. And last, we establish a "minimum bedroom competency," standards that must be met before other, more pleasant things can happen. (In all truthfulness, however, sometimes I just close the door.) We can follow the same procedure for the writing classroom: teach the conventions, check to see that the students know the conventions, and then hold them accountable for producing conventionally correct text. (See Figure 3.8 for an example of how to make this work.)

Feedback by Questioning

When intervention feedback is called for, before offering a solution or a strategy, you can ask the student if he has an idea of what to do. The earlier example of feedback on mathematics problem solving (commenting on the stick figure solution in Sample 2 of Figure 3.7) demonstrates this: "Your strategy worked for part of the problem, but it didn't lead to a correct solution because it fell apart right here. What other strategy could you use to deal with this remaining group of people?" The teacher points out the error, but asks the student to think about how to correct it. Then, if the student draws a blank or describes a nonproductive path, the teacher can provide a suggestion.

To maximize learning, after you have identified an error or problem in students' thinking or work, let them explore how to correct or solve it, before (or instead of) sharing your correction or solution. If their thinking or work demonstrates partial understanding, they may have an idea of what to do about the error or problem; the only intervention they may truly need is a carefully crafted question or two to guide their thought processes.

Figure 3.8

FOR EXAMPLE

Transferring Editing Skills to Students

Editing for correctness requires two things: knowing how to do it correctly and developing the ability to notice it when it is wrong. You can take the following steps to transfer to students the skills and responsibility of error-hunting: teach your students whichever conventions you want them to demonstrate; teach them editor's symbols as a way to identify errors; and then give them practice at using those symbols to hunt for convention mistakes, first in isolation as they learn them and then together with the conventions they have previously learned.

Post a list titled, "Conventions We Have Learned" (or, in the case of older students, "Conventions We Have Had Opportunity to Learn," if you have moved beyond teaching "capital letter at the beginning of a sentence" and "terminal punctuation at the end," but still want to put these targets on the list). Once students have shown they understand the rule for use of the convention and have had practice at error-hunting for it, add it to your list and hold them responsible for finding that problem in their own writing.

If they miss correcting one or more conventions on the next paper they turn in, rather than doing the error-hunting yourself, offer feedback by placing a dot in the margin on the line for each unmarked error and ask them to try again.

This is an example of feedback that points the way to success without going too far: the person who holds the editor's pen does the learning.

Feedback in Discovery Learning Tasks

Not all tasks require an external intervention during the learning. Some tasks, especially in science, are set up as a series of discovery learning events. When corrective are generated through participating in the task itself, feedback from the teacher may take the form of a question or two designed to help students investigate mismatches between prior understanding and present experience. Such questions can be directed to an individual or offered for the class to discuss.

Learning from Errors

Do not use feedback to shortcut learning from errors if a task is structured so that students can analyze their own mistakes and determine a course of action to correct them.

A hallmark of good feedback is that it spurs thoughtful action; it should result in learning, not just following directions or copying someone else's ideas. We are "over-feedbacking" whenever students would benefit from engaging in the thinking that we are doing for them.

5. Effective feedback limits correctives to what students can act on.

When pointing out areas for improvement, first check to see that the student knows what to do with the corrective information she receives. Then, think about how many pieces of advice she can reasonably be expected to act on in the time given. More information than that is overkill. How much feedback is too much is a matter of your professional judgment. Some students can respond to lots of corrective direction without giving up. This recommendation only asks that you differentiate between providing all of the corrective information that would make the work of highest quality and providing as much intervention feedback as the individual student can reasonably act on.

Offering Too Little Corrective Feedback

Do not underestimate students' capacity for taking action and thereby "*under-feedback*"; offer as much corrective feedback as you think they can act on in the time given. (Just keep in mind that identifying *every* problem is not always the most helpful approach for struggling students.)

If student work exhibits a daunting number of problems, you may want to limit the focus of the feedback to one criterion or aspect of quality at a time. This narrows the scope of work for both you and the student. We sometimes offer a great deal of corrective feedback to struggling students, yet if the feedback refers to things they don't know how to do or if it offers too many corrective, it will not be effective. If pointing out every problem with suggestions for how to fix it will overwhelm the student, limit the scope of correctives. Also consider giving students further guided practice opportunities. (See Chapter 5 for more information on focusing on one aspect of quality at a time.)

Suggestions for Offering Feedback

Sometimes quick feedback is all that is needed, but other times a more labor-intensive process is called for. The suggestions that follow offer timesaving strategies that adhere to the requirements for effective feedback.

Picture or Symbol Cues

A metaphor or graphic may help cue your students in how to use your feedback. The following are examples of elementary and secondary applications.

1. Stars and Stairs

Copy a form such as the one in Figure 3.9. Describe what the student did well in the "star" area and offer specific intervention feedback in the "stairs" area. You can also draw the star symbol and the steps symbol next to success and intervention feedback as you write it on their work. (See Appendix B for a reproducible version of Figure 3.9.)

Figure 3.10 shows second-grade teacher Amy Meyer's system for remembering the "stars and stairs" comments she has given to her reading class.

Figure 3.9

Stars and Stairs

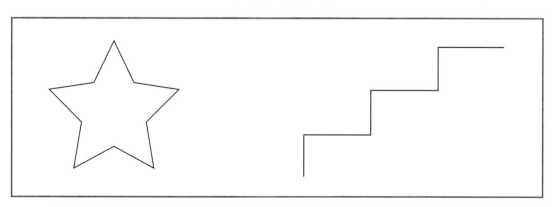

Figure 3.10

Mrs. Meyer's Reading Observations

⌐ *Stair—goal to work on*   ★ *Star—something you do well*

Gabriela	Zoe	Keegan	Chaim
Rereading chapter book for better comprehension	★ *Rereading, Jr. books* ⌐ *Try some new books*	⌐ *Picking "too easy" books* ★ *fluency, retelling*	*sequel → Mouse & Motorcycle* ★ *Great book choices* ★ *Great fiction* ⌐ *Capital letters at beginning of story.*
Gael	**David**	**Brendan**	**Colin**
★ *Chunking a word up* ★ *Getting stuck in a book, recording important facts down in NF* ⌐ *What makes sense?*	★ *Asking ?'s in my head* ⌐ *Stretching out a word—using a stategy* ★ *Good fluency expression!*	★ *Staying with a chapter book, asking ?'s, inferring* ⌐ *Recording think-ing, reading as-signments*	*Discussed determining importance in NF*
Aisha	**Charlie**	**Carmen**	**Eli**
★ *Reading different genres—great pic books* ★ *Asking ?'s* ⌐ *Writing down dif-ferent thinking*	★ *Excellent infer-ences and use of comprehension skills*	★ *fluency, expres-sion, asking ?'s while I read* ⌐ *Skipping over unknown words, trying a strategy*	⌐ *Reread when it doesn't make sense* ★ *Great expression Talks like the char-acters.*
Oscar	**Katherine**	**Marcos**	**Julian**
Geronimo Stilton *Getting recommenda-tions from Chaim*	*Lots of nonfiction webs to record data*	★ *Recording new learning from NF* ⌐ *Tricky words in NF ("pronuncia-tions help")*	★ *Seeing what makes sense Using strategies!* ⌐ *Continue to work on expression* ⌐ *Reread books for fluency*
Abby	**Sophia**	**Austin**	**Peter**
⌐ *1 genre* *Miley/High School Musical* ★ *Great comp., flu-ency*	*What character traits does Amber Brown have?*	★ *Decoding and com-prehension improving!* ⌐ *fluency, expres-sion*	*NF firefighters* ★ *Rereading*

Source: Adapted with permission from Amy Meyer, unpublished classroom materials, Olentangy Local School District, Lewis Center, OH, 2008.

2. *That's Good! Now This*

Record success and intervention feedback on a form such as the one in Figure 3.11, Example 1. If students are resubmitting their work, you may want to use a form such as the one in Example 2. Students revise their work based on your feedback and then reattach the form to their revision with a comment about what they did and a suggestion for what they'd like you to pay particular attention to. This helps you track how they are interpreting your advice. (See Appendix B for reproducible versions of the forms in Figure 3.11.)

Figure 3.11

That's Good! Now This:

Example 1	*Example 2*

That's good!
 	
Now this:
	MY TEACHER'S COMMENTS:
	    That's good!
	
	Now this:
	
	MY COMMENTS:
	    What I did:
	
	    Please give special attention to:

3. *Codes*

Many teachers develop codes to cue corrections, which they write in the margins of student work to indicate what needs fixing up. Foreign language teachers may want to make a list of common errors, create a code, and post it on the wall (e.g., G = gender, T = tense, P = plural, WO = word order). Language arts teachers may want to use an acronym such as CUPS (Capitalization, Usage, Punctuation, and Spelling). To develop a code in your subject area, list errors students commonly make for which a reminder will serve as sufficient direction. Identify a key word in each error and see if your key words will conveniently arrange themselves into an acronym that is pronounceable. If not, either create an easily drawn and remembered symbol for each, or use the first letter of the key word. Post a chart or distribute a key so students can quickly interpret the letter or symbol.

4. *Immediate Feedback for Younger Students*

Preschool teacher Susan Luengen makes laminated charts to test her students on learning targets such as recognizing numbers, shapes, and colors (Figure 3.12). Above each number, shape, or color on the chart, she has affixed a Velcro® dot in a row labeled "Right!" When a child correctly identifies the shape, for example, she gets to attach a Velcro®-backed yellow smiley face above it in the "Right!" row. Mrs. Luengen reports that her children request to do this activity and want to do it over and over, an indicator of how motivating it is for them to watch themselves grow.

Figure 3.12

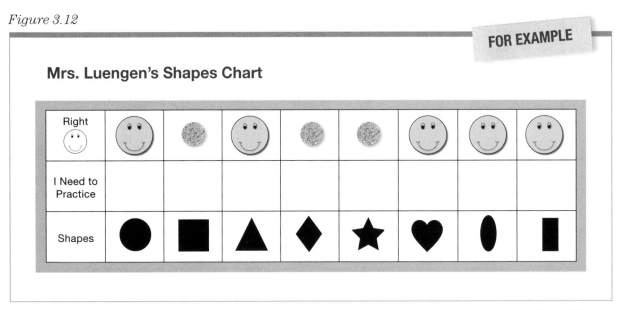

Source: Adapted with permission from Susan Luengen, unpublished classroom materials, Central Oahu School District, Mililani, HI, 2008.

Assessment Dialogues

The previous suggestions are all rather quick forms of feedback. When the focus of the feedback deals with more involved aspects of quality, it can consume a great deal of your time. While we'll probably never get to the point of effective feedback taking none of your time, you can significantly reduce that time by asking students to self-diagnose *before* offering your thoughts. Then you can tailor your comments to offer as much or as little help as the student truly needs. Engaging in this form of "assessment dialogue" can cut down the time you spend formulating feedback—you only need point out successes or problems they overlooked. Options for assessment dialogues described here include written comments, two-color highlighting, and the three-minute conference.

Written Comments

The following written assessment dialogue is structured for use with a performance assessment task and rubric (Stiggins et. al., 2004). It refers to two feedback recording forms, Figure 3.13 for secondary students and Figure 3.14 for elementary students (See Appendix B for reproducible versions of Figures 3.13 and 3.14).

1. Identify a focus for the feedback. Select one or more elements of quality represented on the scoring rubric for the content standard students are working on, based on what you have been teaching. (In general, it is less productive to give feedback on skills or processes for which students have had no instruction.) In some cases, if you have been teaching several facets of quality, you may want to let students determine which one or ones they want to receive feedback on.

2. Students use the scoring rubric to identify their successes (aspects of quality they see in their paper, product, or performance) and one or more aspects of quality that are missing or that they think need work. Encourage them to use the language and concepts of the scoring rubric.

3. Students complete the "My Opinion" portion of the form on Figure 3.13 or Figure 3.14 and turn it in with their work.

4. Review their work and write your feedback in the "Feedback" space, also using the language and/or concepts of the scoring rubric. If you agree with the student, you can write "I agree," but it's always a plus when you can find something she didn't notice to add to the "strengths" comment. You may want to hold a personal conference with or plan a small-group lesson for those students whose opinions differ significantly from yours.

5. After receiving your feedback, students take their own opinions and your comments into account and decide what to do next, creating a specific plan for further work focused on ideas or strategies that will improve the paper, product, or performance. Some students will be able to complete it on their own; others will need your help, at least at first.

Figure 3.13

Assessment Dialogue Form

Name: _____ Date: _____

Assignment: _____ Feedback Focus: _____

MY OPINION

My strengths are _____

_____

What I think I need to work on is _____

_____

_____

FEEDBACK

Strengths: _____

_____

_____

Work on: _____

_____

_____

MY PLAN

What I will do now: _____

_____

_____

_____

_____

Source: Adapted with permission from S. Chappuis, R. Stiggins, J. Arter, and J. Chappuis, *Assessment* FOR *Learning: An Action Guide for School Leaders* (Portland, OR: ETS Assessment Training Institute, 2004), p. 193.

Figure 3.14

Assessment Dialogue Form for Younger Students

Name: _____ Date: _____

Assignment: _____ Feedback Focus: _____

MY OPINION

★ My strengths are _____

_____

What I think I need to work on is _____

_____

_____

MY TEACHER'S FEEDBACK

★ Strengths: _____

_____

Work on: _____

_____

_____

MY PLAN

What I will do now: _____

_____

_____

_____

_____

If your students tend to set large, nonspecific, or performance goals instead of identifying next steps ("My plan is to do better" or "My plan is to get an A"), redirect them to your intervention feedback if it offered pointers centering on actions likely to improve their work, or provide additional suggestions.

Two-color Highlighting

Another possibility (Shannon Thompson, personal communication, 2001) is to dispense with the assessment dialogue form and have students mark with a yellow highlighter the phrases on the scoring rubric that they think describe their work. They turn the highlighted scoring rubric in with their work, and you mark with a blue highlighter the phrases that you believe describe it. Where you and the student are in agreement, the phrases are green. Phrases that remain yellow and blue represent areas where you and the student differ.

You can offer additional written comments for those students whose opinions vary significantly from yours, or you can meet with them individually or in small groups, depending on the learning they need to do. Students can also highlight a developmental continuum or other graphic display that describes elements of quality, as long as the wording is suitable for their use (they understand the terms and the document does not use negative evaluative labels, such as "failing" or "far below standard").

The Three-minute Conference

You can use the assessment dialogue process to provide oral feedback to one or more students individually. Some teachers, particularly in the primary grades, do structure time to meet with each student regularly. If you do not have the opportunity to do this, you may still want to meet with certain students while others are working independently or engaged in peer conferences. To minimize the time an individual conference can take, have the student self-assess prior to the conference, filling out the "My Opinion" portion of the Assessment Dialogue form (see Figures 3.13 and 3.14).

At the beginning of the conference, ask the student to share his thoughts. Then share your feedback. If appropriate, point out a strength the student overlooked and add to or modify what the student said he needs to work on. Let him be the writer on the Assessment Dialogue form, even for your comments. Many teachers find that when students think about their work first, these conferences can be successfully completed in three minutes or less.

Regardless of how you deliver descriptive feedback, consider asking students to engage in self-assessment prior to receiving your feedback. Students' reflecting on their work increases the likelihood that they will understand your feedback and act on it. This is an example of *accessing prior knowledge*, which helps students make sense of new information and retain it longer. In addition, it communicates that they have an equal responsibility in thinking about quality. It teaches students that their opinions are welcomed and respected. And, when students speak first, you are better able to identify misconceptions and target comments to what they can't figure out for themselves.

Offering Feedback with a Scoring Rubric

Make sure you have introduced the language of the rubric (Strategy 1) in advance of using it to offer feedback. Students will understand your comments better if you have also given them practice with Strategy 2, evaluating strong and weak anonymous samples, which helps them internalize the concepts of quality described in the rubric.

If your students aren't used to expressing their thoughts about their work before hearing from you, let them know in advance that you will be asking them to do so. Some students don't like surprises—you want this to be a challenge they are comfortable attempting.

Peer Feedback

In a study of the effects of peer- and self-assessment on science achievement, White and Frederiksen (1998) found that the process of coming to understand the criteria by which their work would be judged and learning to apply it to their own and to others' work benefited all students and worked to narrow the achievement gap between low- and high-achieving students. (See Figure 4.1 in Chapter 4 for a summary of White and Frederiksen's study.)

Although finding time for students to give feedback to each other can be difficult, several learning advantages make it worth the effort. First, when students practice constructing descriptive feedback for their peers, they deepen their own understanding of quality. Second, if students are trained to recognize and describe features of quality, they can offer valuable constructive critiques to each other, which lightens your load as a teacher. Third, some students are more relaxed and receptive to feedback from a peer, who is not in the position of "expert" that you occupy. Fourth, because they themselves are engaged in completing the assignment, students can often come up with strategies for tackling problems their peers are struggling with. Fifth, after conferring with a peer, they are more likely to attempt to view their work through another's eyes, which can trigger new thoughts and insights into what to rework. And last, it taps into the advantages that social interaction can contribute to learning.

White and Frederiksen (1998) describe two prerequisites to engaging students in peer feedback activities, based on their studies of reflective assessment (peer- and self-assessment) in the science classroom:

1. All participants must understand that it is performance that is being rated, not people, where performance is what you actually do, not what you are capable of doing.

2. Students must be given the means to understand how to do well in their performances; otherwise performance ratings may be damaging to students.

> These caveats relate to a very serious issue: Reflective assessment [peer- and self-assessment] can be seen as a performance evaluation if it occurs in an instructional context that teaches students how to carry out good inquiry projects. However, if the process of producing a high-quality project is mysterious to students, they are likely to fall back on an ability attribution for the assessment results, that is, on the belief that they are not "smart enough" to do well in science. There is a clear equity issue here as well, because failure to provide both an understanding of the assessment criteria and of how to perform well may be particularly damaging to less-advantaged students who, without a clear understanding of how highly rated work is produced, are likely to invoke the damaging theory of performance as a reflection of their ability. So, reflective assessment should not be added on to a curriculum, rather it should be an integral part of a curriculum that scaffolds the development of the skills being assessed. (pp. 79–80)

Scaffolding a Peer Feedback Conference

You can teach students to give feedback to each other by having them practice in a controlled setting. Limiting the variables "scaffolds" the experience so they can focus on mastering the basics first.

One way to accomplish this is to have them engage in a three-minute conference simulation with a partner, in which they take turns playing the roles of student and teacher. Select two anonymous samples of student work that each fall in the midrange of quality, illustrating strengths and areas needing attention for the aspect or aspects of quality you want students to focus on in their own works in progress. Label the samples "Student A" and "Student B." If students do not already have a copy of the scoring rubric they will use to practice giving feedback with, prepare a copy for each one. They will also each need a copy of the Assessment Dialogue form in Figure 3.13 or 3.14 and scratch paper. Then follow this process:

1. Ask students to find a partner. The person with the longer fingers is "Partner A." The other person is "Partner B." Tell students that for the first activity, "Partner A" is the student and "Partner B" is the teacher.

2. Hand out (or ask them to take out) the scoring rubric. If it is a multi-trait rubric, direct their attention to the trait or traits they are to focus on. Give them a few minutes to review it.

3. Hand out the sample labeled "Student A" and tell them that Partner A has just completed this piece of work. They are to take a few minutes independently to read through it, compare it to the rubric, and find words and phrases that they think describe what they see. Give them enough time to read the sample and review the rubric. Partner A writes her thoughts on the Assessment Dialogue form (Figure 3.13 or 3.14). Partner B writes his thoughts on scratch paper. (Alternatively, you can have them mark phrases on the scoring rubric, but you will have to have separate copies for each activity.)

4. When all are ready, ask them to conduct a three-minute conference with their partners. Partner A speaks first. When it's Partner B's turn to speak, Partner A writes B's comments on the Assessment Dialogue form.

5. While they are talking with each other, walk around the room and look for students who are using the language of quality and students who seem to be struggling. Make note of where problems seem to be if they don't quite have the hang of it yet. Address the problems in general terms after the first simulation, before beginning the second one. ("Some of you seemed to struggle a bit with _____. What did you notice?"; "How might we solve that problem? What are some things you can do?")

6. Time their conferences—give them a two-minute reminder and then let them know when three minutes are up. Ask them to thank their partners.

7. Then you can have partners discuss what "Student A" could do next, either by working together to fill out the "My Plan" portion of the Assessment Dialogue form or as a large-group exploration of strategies that might improve the work.

8. You may want to conduct a brief discussion at this point if you noticed some problems at step 5.

9. Repeat the process with the second sample, labeled "Student B," where Partner B is the student and Partner A is the teacher.

10. Debrief the process by taking five minutes to ask students questions such as these:

   - What was easy about this? What was hard?
   - What did you discover when you were being the student? What did you learn when you were being the teacher?
   - What did this teach you about _____ (the elements of quality they were focused on)?
   - How would you describe the characteristics of helpful feedback?

In certain contexts, such as mathematics problem solving, before engaging in a three-minute conference simulation, students should attempt to solve the problem themselves. Then they put their own work aside and participate in the simulation with anonymous samples. At the conclusion, they can review their own solutions and make any changes they think of after having discussed the two samples.

What does engaging in the simulation do for students? It acclimates them to the idea that they might think first about their work before asking someone else to look it over. It prepares them to give feedback to others, and it causes them to think more deeply about the elements of quality they are learning.

Students can use the same process to seek and offer feedback from one another. The peer conference version of the Assessment Dialogue form found in Appendix B includes a line in which they can request further feedback either from a specific person or choose between "teacher" and "peer" (where you assign the partners), depending on your preference.

Evidence suggests that in peer feedback situations, struggling learners benefit from heterogeneous pairing or grouping, while stronger students do well in either homogenous or heterogeneous groups (White & Frederiksen, 1998). So, consider assigning heterogeneous partners or groups of three or four members, at least until the struggling students are performing more successfully.

About Peer Editing . . .

If you have students edit each other's work for issues of correctness, consider requiring that they first have reviewed their own papers and have found all the errors they are capable of finding. The argument for peer editing (and it is valid, in my opinion) is that in life beyond school, we ask others to check over our work when correctness counts. Let us model in-school peer editing after beyond-school practice: we don't ask others to do our work for us—we check it first. To let students hand over the complete editing task to someone else encourages a bad habit—expecting someone else to do their work.

Making Sure Students Understand the Language of Quality

If students are not comfortable with the concepts included in your scoring rubric (or other definition of quality you will ultimately use to judge their work), they won't be able to give each other useful feedback reliably, so make sure they have engaged in some version of Strategies 1 and 2 prior to engaging in this Strategy 3 activity.

If you have taught students editors' symbols, they can use them to mark errors on one another's papers, but hold the original author responsible for making the changes.

Sometimes, having students peer edit is not recommended. Although every paper does not have to be edited entirely by the author, in English class you need to evaluate each student's usage of spelling, punctuation, grammar, and capitalization periodically within the context of their writing. Peer editing masks individual achievement because it is a joint effort. If you teach English, keep in mind that there are times in life beyond school when we have to produce the best version of error-free text we are capable of, independent of others, and help students develop this capability by teaching them to edit solo.

When writing conventions are not the focus of the achievement to be demonstrated, encourage students to use peer editors.

Peer Response Groups

You may want to broaden the experience by expanding from partner feedback to small-group feedback. Think of peer feedback in group settings as "assessment conversations" that students have with one another. Set the stage for these conversations by establishing norms or guidelines for how they will take place: what protocol students are to follow, kinds of comments likely to be most helpful, how to offer feedback, and how to respond when receiving it.

Here is an example of a procedure based on how a writing response group functions, which can be adapted to peer feedback groups responding to written work in any content area. Groups of three or four members generally work best; they provide some diversity of opinion and can complete the process in 20 to 30 minutes.

1. All members come prepared to read their work in progress. This means they are prepared to give it a good interpretive reading to showcase the ideas as clearly as possible.

2. Before reading, each person identifies what aspects of quality he or she would like feedback on. Ideally, they relate to concepts in the scoring rubric or other mutually understood characteristics. What specifically should members listen for?

3. When one person is reading, every one else listens.

4. The author reads through once. Other group members listen without commenting. At the end of the reading, group members take a few minutes to jot down thoughts. (This is an optional step, but helpful for the group to think more clearly about the piece as a whole).

5. The author reads through a second time. Group members take notes, focusing on the feedback requested.

6. Group members either share their thoughts orally or write them down. If written, they can share them right after the author has read or save them until all have finished reading and then read comments at the end. Figure 3.15 shows a sample peer response recording form. (See Appendix B for a reproducible version of Figure 3.15.)

Suggestions for Students in Peer Response Groups

Here are some suggestions for what you might tell students when they are receiving peer feedback (derived in part from Spandel, 2009):

1. Think about what you want the group to pay attention to—what do you want feedback on? Let your group know. For example, if you have questions about how to handle an idea or where to take it, ask for suggestions.

Figure 3.15

Peer Response Feedback Sheet

Date: _____

Author: _____

Title: _____

Feedback Requested: _____

My response: _____

_____

2. Give your paper the best reading you can so that your group can really visualize what you are saying.

3. Don't apologize. You want the group to offer honest responses about your work. "Just plunge in. . . . Be brave. Read your text with confidence so that the feedback you get will be more about your writing and less about you" (Spandel, 2009, p. 360).

4. Thank group members for their comments. Don't argue with them. It's okay if you don't agree with them, but you don't have to tell them that. Think of their comments as gifts—some gifts you use and some you put away, but you always thank the giver. You are in charge of your work, so you get to decide which comments to act on. Even if you don't think you will use the comment, say thank you.

Here are some suggestions for what you might tell students when they are giving feedback:

1. Use your best listening skills: first, listen to what the author wants feedback on and then keep that in mind as you listen to him read.

2. You are offering the author the gift of an audience response to her ideas. Positive feedback isn't always praise. Sometimes it's an honest response that shares what her ideas caused you to see, to understand, to feel, or to think differently about.

3. If you have a question or a suggestion to offer, phrase it as an "I" statement: "I felt confused when . . ."; "I wondered why . . ."; "I wanted to know more about. . . ." If your first thought begins with "You need to . . .", you have come up with a solution to a problem. Think about the *question in your mind* that triggered your solution idea and offer the *question* as feedback. Comments that help the author figure out what needs work can be even more valuable than comments that tell the author what to do (unless that is what he has asked for).

4. Remember that the author is in charge of the quality of the paper. Your feedback doesn't have to fix everything. Your role is to offer your thoughts respectfully.

Figure 3.16 describes how a high school English department conducts peer feedback sessions, and Figure 3.17 gives subject-specific suggestions for using peer feedback.

Figure 3.16

FOR EXAMPLE

Peer Review in High School English Classes

In grades 9–12 (in our school), individual teachers tend to have their own way to handle peer review, but there are some universal trends. Typically, peer review is used to create student learning conversations during the middle phase of the writing process. For some teachers, once students have working drafts, they meet in partnerships or small teams to review their work. The review process is focused on ideas and content, organization and structure, and voice. Many teachers adapt the 6+1 trait rubric so that it can be used by the kids to formatively assess the work of their peers.

After providing time in class to review, students use the comments to revise their drafts. At this time, many teachers formally collect the revised drafts (or specific paragraphs) to offer their comments. When the paper is returned, students use the teacher's comments (and writing conferences) to start working on their final drafts. Several days before the due date, students get back in their peer review partnerships/groups and look at their essays again. This time grammar and conventions are evaluated along with the other traits. Throughout the process, students complete metacognitive reflection tasks that ask them to think about the strengths and weaknesses of their drafts. Our Creative Writing class uses a workshop approach that involves one full week per unit devoted to peer review.

Source: Used with permission from Michael L. Doman, Naperville Community Unit School District 203, Naperville, IL, 2009.

Figure 3.17

FOR EXAMPLE

Subject-specific Peer Feedback Applications

Mathematics: Students can critique each other's extended problem solutions. Let them read through each other's solutions and explanations and then offer comments on whichever aspects of quality you (or they) select as the focus. They can use a student-friendly scoring rubric to guide their critiques. For example, if the focus is Mathematical Communication, they can give feedback on clarity and completeness of the explanation and correct usage of mathematical terms.

Science: Students may be working on a project that demonstrates their mastery of the inquiry process. Depending on the requirements of the task, they may either read their work aloud or exchange work with another student for feedback on one or more characteristics of quality. They also will need a student-friendly scoring rubric or explicit list of criteria to guide their critiques (e.g., formulating an hypothesis; designing and conducting an investigation; gathering, analyzing, and interpreting data; communicating results [National Research Council, 1996]).

Social studies: Students may be working on a paper that compares and contrasts two religions they are studying. It will be very important here as well that they have a student-friendly scoring rubric or explicit list of criteria that offers a clear notion of what constitutes quality as it relates to social studies knowledge and reasoning learning targets (e.g., presents accurate factual information, chooses appropriate things to compare, chooses appropriate characteristics on which to base comparisons, identifies similarities and differences accurately, explains similarities and differences with sufficient detail [Marzano, Pickering, & McTighe, 1993]).

Writing: Younger students can begin by looking or listening for one thing: a phrase that sparks their imagination, a surprising word, a catchy beginning, a stretchy sentence. Model this for them by first pointing out characteristics of good writing in what you read aloud to them: "I noticed. . . ." Invite them to offer their own observations: "What did you notice?" Then move to identifying those characteristics in examples of student writing (not from them). Ask them for suggestions of what they might notice in their classmates' writing and what they might like to have others notice in theirs. Let them practice on anonymous student work, before trying it with a partner. Debrief by asking them what feelings and thoughts the experience elicited.

Tips for Timing

It's helpful to think carefully in advance about how much time you will allow for students to participate in peer response groups. To make the process as efficient as possible, consider these suggestions:

- Students don't need to share the whole piece of work if they only need or want feedback on a portion of it.

- Keep feedback groups fairly small—three to four students per group. This process takes time and the more students in a group, the longer it will take.

- Give students a timeframe for each portion of the process. How long should each member spend presenting his work? How long for group members to compose their responses? How long for sharing their responses?

Conclusion

Teaching students to see their work as opportunities to improve is at the heart of learning. When we offer feedback effectively, students greet assessment information warmly, because it builds a hopeful vision: "I think I can do this"—rather than establishing a dreaded, fatalistic sense: "Here I go again, down the drain grade-wise for another year." We can model an open, forward-looking stance to learning through how we respond to their work and then we can show them how to look at their own work in the same way.

CHAPTER 4

Where Am I Now?
Self-assessment and Goal Setting

Strategy 4
Teach students to self-assess and set goals.

Strategy 4
Teach students to self-assess and set goals.

When students are involved in self-assessment, they provide themselves with regular and immediate descriptive feedback to guide their learning. They become more actively involved in a curriculum that otherwise can seem unrelated to their lives and personal experiences.

—*Gregory, Cameron, & Davies, 2000, p. 10*

"*H*ow'm I doin'?" "Well, it looks FINE to me." "I AM done." "Is this what you want?" The best defense against confusion about quality is a good offense. By offering descriptive feedback we model for students the kind of thinking we want them to engage in when looking at their own work. The next logical step is to hand over that skill and responsibility. When students self-assess and set goals they develop an internal sense of control over the conditions of their success and greater ownership of the responsibility for improving. Engaging in self-assessment and goal setting can also cause students to value descriptive feedback more highly than the grade. But, students' self-assessments are sometimes inaccurate and the goals they set can be ineffective or unwieldy. In this chapter, we'll look at research on both self-assessment and goal setting and provide strategies for teaching students how to do them well.

"Formative assessment requires that pupils have a central part in it . . . . [U]nless they come to understand their strengths and weaknesses, and how they might deal with them, they will not make progress."

Harlen & James, 1997, p. 372

Impact of Self-assessment on Student Achievement

The good news is, if you have made the intended learning clear to students and have had them practice self-assessment as you have given descriptive feedback, the transition to accurately evaluating the strengths and weaknesses of their own work won't be difficult. Even though finding time for students to self-assess and set goals for improvement can be challenging, the benefits to learning are worth it. These practices do increase achievement and motivation.

In one study described by Black & Wiliam (1998a), elementary students with learning difficulties received one of three forms of feedback on their oral reading rates: feedback from the teacher, feedback from their peers, or self-generated feedback. Black & Wiliam report, "The largest gains, measured by comparison of pre- and post-test scores over the programme's period of nine weeks, were achieved by the self-monitoring group, whilst all three did better than a control group who had no formative feedback. . . . [T]he peer and self-monitoring methods were preferred (by teachers and students) and one benefit of both was that they reduced the amount of time that the special education teachers had to spend on measurement in their classroom" (p. 27).

In another study, with middle school science students, White and Frederiksen (1998) tested the effects of what they call "Reflective Assessment," a cycle of peer- and self-assessment, on scientific inquiry skills. They found that "students' learning was greatly facilitated by Reflective Assessment. Furthermore, adding this metacognitive process to the curriculum was particularly beneficial for low-achieving students: Performance on their research projects and inquiry tests was significantly closer to that of high-achieving students than was the case in the control classes. Thus, this approach has the valuable effect of reducing the educational disadvantage of low-achieving students while also being beneficial for high-achieving students. We argue that these findings have strong implications for what such metacognitively focused, inquiry-oriented curricula can accomplish, particularly in urban school settings in which there are many disadvantaged students" (p. 4). Figure 4.1 presents a summary of White and Frederiksen's study.

Providing students with opportunities for a combination of peer feedback and self-assessment causes them to achieve at significantly higher levels, without more instruction. These two practices increase their sense of ownership of the responsibility to learn. And the time you spend offering feedback lessens as students' self-assessment skills grow.

Figure 4.1

RESEARCH SNAPSHOT

"Inquiry, Modeling, and Metacognition:
Making Science Accessible to All Students"

White & Frederiksen, 1998

Hypothesis:
Students' ability to engage in scientific inquiry will be enhanced by the addition of a metacognitive process in which students reflect on their own and each other's learning.

Who Was Involved:
Twelve urban classes of students in grades 7 through 9, classified as high achieving or low achieving on the basis of their combined CTBS verbal and quantitative test scores.

What They Did:
The researchers first developed a program using the scientific inquiry cycle to teach middle school students to design and create causal models of force and motion (the ThinkerTools Inquiry Curriculum). Participating classes were divided into two groups—a "Reflective Assessment" group and a control group. Both groups received the same instruction and completed the same activities, engaging in the inquiry cycle through seven modules scaffolded to develop understanding of how forces affect motion. They all completed two inquiry research projects, one after the third module and the other after the seventh. Students were free to choose their partners in working on the research projects—some research groups were composed of high-achieving students, some were composed of low-achieving students, and some were a mixture of both.

The "Reflective Assessment" group participated in a cycle of reflective peer- and self-assessment. They were first introduced to a set of criteria for good

Figure 4.1 (continued)

scientific research at the beginning of the curriculum. Then, at the end of each phase of the inquiry cycle in each module, students evaluated their work using the most relevant criteria. At the end of each module, they evaluated the work for all criteria. In addition, when they presented their research projects to the class, they evaluated their own and gave each other feedback orally and in writing.

What the Researchers Found:

- In the Reflective Assessment classes, the gap between low-achieving and high-achieving students' performance on research projects and inquiry tests was significantly narrower than it was in the control classes (p. 34).

- On a test of inquiry skills, the average gain for students in the Reflective Assessment classes was three times that of the control classes. An analysis of subscores reveals the greatest gains came from the most difficult aspects of the test (pp. 48–49).

- Low-achieving students (CTBS composite <60) in the Reflective Assessment classes performed almost as well on their research projects as high-achieving students (CTBS composite >60) in the control classes (p. 51).

- Low-achieving students in Reflective Assessment classes benefited from heterogeneous grouping (p. 38).

Source: Summarized from B. Y. White & J. R. Frederiksen, "Inquiry, Modeling, and Metacognition: Making Science Accessible to All Students," *Cognition and Instruction, 16*(1), 1998, 3–118.

Three Parts: Self-assessment, Justification, and Goal Setting

Strategy 4 has three parts. The first is self-assessment, where students make judgments about what they know, have learned, or have mastered. The second is justification, where students show evidence in their work as rationale for their judgments. The third is goal setting, where students make a plan for continued learning. All three do not have to be present at all times—it depends on the context. It may be most appropriate for students to do only a quick self-assessment, especially for simpler learning targets, and you may be the one planning further action on the basis of their information. Sometimes students will interpret the results of an assessment you have evaluated; other times they will be doing the evaluation themselves. And in some contexts, students may be responsible for planning further action. In the following sections, you will see activities that include one or more of the three parts of this strategy in various combinations.

 Directing Attention to the Learning

Self-assessment and goal-setting processes and forms should direct attention to improving features of the work as they relate to the learning targets (a learning goal), rather than to getting a better score or grade (a performance goal). If students do the learning, the grade will follow.

Quick Self-assessment Ideas

The following suggestions are fairly simple to carry out and don't take much time. The first few are suited to primary students, the majority are aimed at elementary and middle school students, and a few can be used across grade levels.

1. Young children can move checkers, buttons, or poker chips to track learning. Each time a child moves a checker, button, or chip, she is celebrating a bit of progress. For young students who require immediate gratification or who haven't yet made the connection between effort and success, simple concrete actions can be helpful. A student can put a button on a string for every spelling word mastered. Or, you can put checkers in a jar, each representing a different learning target and have students move the checkers into a different jar as they master each learning target (Donna Snodgrass, Cleveland State University, personal communication, 2005).

2. Primary students can make learning chains by creating learning links from a template such as the one shown in Figure 4.2. (See Appendix B for a reproducible version of Figure 4.2.) When students have mastered a learning target, let them complete a link and save it in an envelope or bag. Periodically have students tape their links together and add them to a class chain. Each link makes an equal contribution to the total length of the chain no matter whether the links represent the work of the most advanced student or the work of a student who is just starting to make progress. You can make color-coded chains, with each color representing either a subject for a multi-subject class chain or a learning target for a subject-specific chain (Donna Snodgrass, Cleveland State University, personal communication, 2005).

Figure 4.2

Learning Chains

Reserve for taping

Reserve for taping

Name: _____   Date: _____

I have learned to: _____

_____

Evidence: _____

_____

Source: Adapted with permission from Donna Snodgrass, unpublished classroom materials, Cleveland State University, Cleveland, OH, 2005.

3. With elementary-age students, if you have used "Stars and Stairs" to offer success and intervention feedback, you can explain self-assessment and goal setting in the same terms: "What have I done well? That's my star." and "What can I do next? That's my stair." What's the difference between "stars" and "stairs"? The letter *I*. "What step am I going to take to reach the star?" Students can write their "stars" and "stairs" on a form such as Figure 3.9 in Chapter 3 (also reproduced in Appendix B).

4. Students can also use a "Stamping Stairs" form such as the one in Figure 4.3, where they stamp and date their progress on one learning target, from "Just beginning" to "Success." (See Appendix B for a reproducible version of Figure 4.3.)

5. Use the "KWL" strategy. At the beginning of a unit, have students draw three columns on a piece of paper, labeled "K," "W," and "L." Ask students what they already *know* about the topic(s) and have them write that in the "K" column. Then ask them what they *want* to learn and have them write that in the "W" column. At the end of the unit, ask them what they *learned* and have them write it in the "L" column. Here is a variation on the "KWL" activity (Gregory, Cameron, & Davies, 2000):

> Give students a blank sheet of paper (11" x 17") before you begin a new unit of study. Have students sketch, write, or diagram anything they think they already know on the topic. Collect these sheets. Partway through the unit, return the sheets to the students and ask them to add information they now know on the topic using a different colour of ink. At the end of the unit, repeat the process. (p. 25)

Figure 4.3

Stamping Stairs

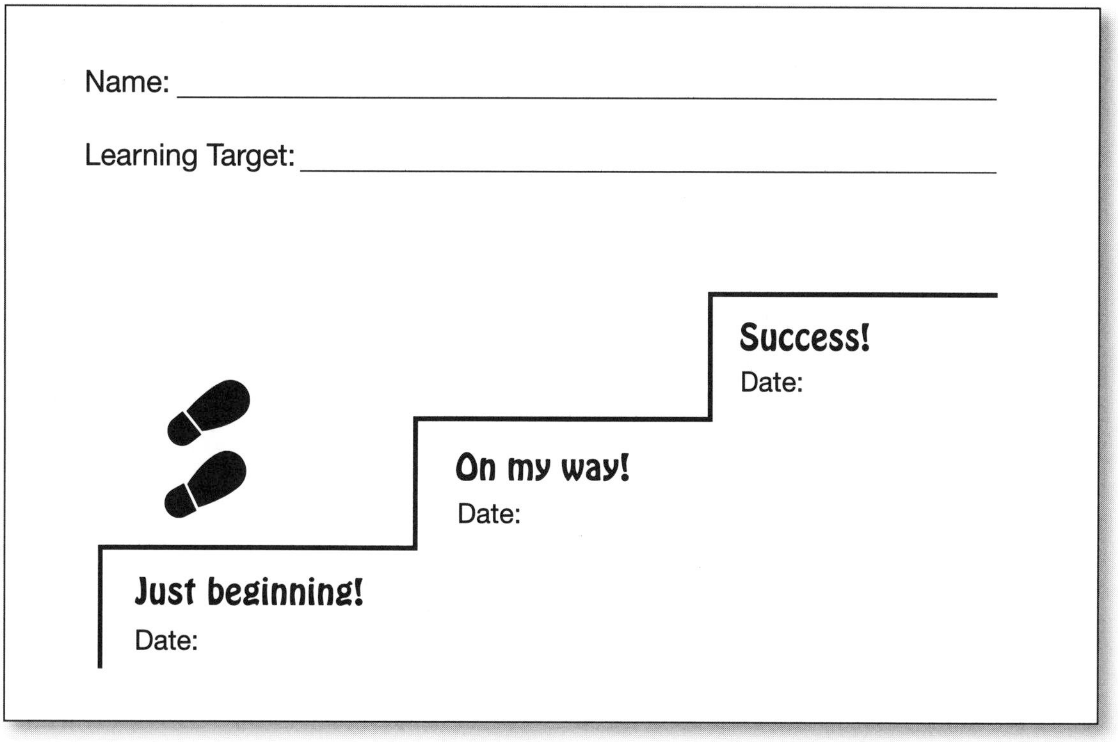

Name: _____

Learning Target: _____

Success!
Date:

On my way!
Date:

Just beginning!
Date:

6. If at the outset of a unit you give learning targets to students in the form of "I am learning . . ." statements ("I am learning how other civilizations influenced the development of Greek civilization"), students can write an "I am learning" statement as an "I can" statement when they have mastered the target ("I can explain how other civilizations might have influenced the development of Greek civilization") and staple it to the evidence.

7. Students can keep a list of the learning targets for a grading period and regularly mark the ones they have mastered.

8. Students can complete an exit task at the end of a lesson to assess their level of understanding and turn it in before leaving. This closure activity deepens awareness of the intended learning and you can use the information to inform instruction for the next lesson (Sue Cho & Aaron Mukai, Mukilteo School District, Everett, WA, personal communication, 2008). Figure 4.4 shows an example of a mathematics exit task.

Figure 4.4

FOR EXAMPLE

Diameter-Circumference Exit Task

Name: _____

Today's Learning Target:
I can explain the relationship between the diameter and circumference of a circle.

Self-assessment: _____

_____

Evidence:
Samantha was measuring circles around her home. The diameter of her little sister's bicycle wheel is 12 inches. Predict the circumference. **Be sure to clearly explain why you think your prediction make sense.**

_____

_____

_____

Source: Used with permission from Sue Cho and Aaron Mukai, unpublished classroom materials, Mukilteo School District, Everett, WA, 2008.

9. Students can write a letter (on paper or via email) to their parents about a piece of work, explaining where they are now with it and what they are trying to do next.

10. Before or during a unit of study, ask students to categorize their understanding of concepts using "traffic light" icons. They mark their work with a green, yellow, or red dot to indicate good, partial, or little understanding. Students can discuss their judgments in small groups and explain their rationale. You can have students with green and yellow dots work together while you conduct a lesson for students with red dots (Black, Harrison, Lee, Marshall, & Wiliam, 2002).

Self-assessment and Goal Setting with Selected Response and Constructed Response Tasks

The following ideas take students more deeply into thinking about their learning. They work well when students are focusing on knowledge and reasoning learning targets and are demonstrating their achievement with selected response items and short constructed response tasks.

Before: Targeting the Learning

Students can self-assess and set goals for learning, either before the learning by analyzing pretest results, or before taking a test by deciding which targets they have mastered and which ones they still need to work on.

1. Using Pretest Results

If you give a pretest to students, you can prepare a chart that shows which learning target each item on the test measures and then hand it out along with the corrected test. Have students use the chart to identify which targets they already know and which they need to learn, based on how they did on each item. You will need to make sure that you have sampled each target sufficiently on the pretest for this to be a valid judgment. (For more information on how to construct accurate selected response tests, see Stiggins et al., 2004, Chapter 5.) Figure 4.5 illustrates this activity with a middle school mathematics pretest.

 Match to Content Standards

The items on a formative quiz or test should match the learning targets you are teaching. If it's not clear which learning target an item is intended to assess, rewrite the item or delete it.

2. Highlighting Targets

Before beginning a unit, or a few days prior to a test, have students use highlighters to mark a list of learning targets to be taught in the unit or represented on the test. Students highlight in green those they believe they have mastered, yellow those they think need a little review with, and red those they are the most unsure of having mastered. You can use this information to plan instruction, or students can create a plan identifying what they will do to study the yellow and red highlighted learning targets.

Figure 4.5

FOR EXAMPLE

Self-assessment and Goal Setting with Pretest Results

Fraction Study — Plan of Action

Fraction Study Targets:

- I will use factors to rewrite fractions in lowest terms.

- I will use common denominators to compare, order, add, and subtract fractions.

- I will use the relationship between fractions and mixed numbers to add, subtract, multiply, and divide fractions.

Lesson Targets	Pre-assessment Results					Plan of Action
	# Right	# Wrong	Simple Errors	👍	👎	
Fractions to Lowest Terms						What is your strength?
Fraction Multiplication						What is your specific target (weakness)?
Fractions to Mixed #						
Mixed # to Fraction						Who will help you reach your target?
Order/Compare Fractions						
Fraction/Mixed # Addition						
Fraction/Mixed # Subtraction						
Mixed # Multiplication						
Fraction/Mixed # Division						

Source: Adapted with permission from Paula Smith, unpublished classroom materials, Naperville Community Unit School District 203, Naperville, IL, 2009.

3. Ranking with a Scale

Students can also estimate their level of mastery for each target using a ranking scale and then form study groups based on the results. First, make a numbered list of the learning targets students are working on and provide a ranking scale such as one of these:

1 = I don't know this very well yet.

2 = I need a little review on this.

3 = I know this well.

Or

1 = I'm just beginning—I don't know how to do any of this.

2 = I've made a little progress—I know a little bit about how to do this.

3 = I'm halfway home—I can do some parts of this well.

4 = I'm almost there—I know how to do this pretty well.

5 = I made it—I'm confident that I can do this very well.

Have students rate their current level of mastery on the learning target list. Figure 4.6 shows an example of this activity using the mathematics learning targets from the pretest in Figure 4.5.

You can then target instruction with one of the following activities:

- Conduct one or more small-group reviews focused on specific learning targets for students who have identified those targets as areas of need—students can self-select into the reviews. Other students can work independently reviewing material for the test.

- Offer suggestions for each learning target: "To review learning target number 1, reread pages 246 to 250 and do problems 1 and 2 on page 251." Encourage students to select which work they need to do.

- Have students assign themselves to study groups based on their greatest needs and offer suggested activities for each group, either to be conducted in class or outside of class.

Figure 4.6

Where Am I Now?

Directions:

Evaluate your own level of mastery on each of the learning targets listed below according to the following scale:

1 = I'm just beginning—I don't know how to do any of this.

2 = I've made a little progress—I know a little bit about how to do this.

3 = I'm halfway home—I can do some parts of this well.

4 = I'm almost there—I know how to do this pretty well.

5 = I made it—I'm confident that I can do this very well.

Learning Targets	Rating
1. Converting fractions to lowest terms	
2. Multiplying fractions	
3. Converting fractions to mixed numbers	
4. Converting mixed numbers to fractions	
5. Ordering and comparing fractions	
6. Adding fractions and mixed numbers	
7. Subtracting fractions and mixed numbers	
8. Multiplying mixed numbers	
9. Dividing fractions and mixed numbers	

Figure 4.7 shows a variation created by middle school mathematics teachers Sue Cho and Aaron Mukai. Here is how they describe its use and the effects on their students (personal communication, 2008):

> This self-assessment is given at the beginning of the unit along with a pre-assessment that allows students to set goals for the unit. It also allows us to formatively assess them to help plan and modify lessons. Students also self-assess at the end of the unit to reflect on their progress. [In using this] we have noticed students are better able to understand what it is they know or need to improve. Students now set goals for the unit and strive to achieve their goals by working hard to understand the material

and asking thinking questions when they are struggling. Our students are now more relaxed and confident on the summative assessments because they know what is expected of them.

Figure 4.7

Properties of a Circle Self-assessment

Self-assessment Rubric			
4 – Exceeds	3 – Meets	2 – Approaching	1 – Below
I have a complete understanding of the learning target and I can apply and extend the concept to new situations.	I have a complete understanding of the learning target.	I have some understanding of the learning target.	I don't understand the learning target.

POWER STANDARD: Understand the properties of circles.	
Learning Target	Self-assessment
I can use the radius to find the diameter of a circle.	
I can use the diameter to find the radius of a circle.	
I can explain the relationship between the diameter and circumference of a circle.	
I can explain why the formula, C = diameter x π works for finding the circumference of a circle.	
I can use the circumference to find the diameter of a circle.	
I can explain why the formula, A = radius^2 x π works for finding the area of a circle.	

Source: Used with permission from Sue Cho and Aaron Mukai, unpublished classroom materials, Mukilteo School District, Everett, WA, 2008.

4. Human Bar Graph

In this activity, students estimate their level of mastery, as in the preceding activity, and then form a human bar graph for each learning target, which you can then use to identify which concepts to review as a large group. First, have students do the following:

- Self-assess using a form such as one of those shown in the preceding activity.

- Take a blank sheet of paper and number it so that it corresponds to the number of learning targets on the list (e.g., if there are nine separate learning targets, they will number from one to nine). Students don't put their names on this paper. It is anonymous.

- Transfer their personal rankings for each target to the numbered paper. Remind them not to put their names on this paper.

- Crumple their numbered paper into a ball about the size of a snowball, form a circle, and toss their snowballs at one another. They continue picking up and tossing snowballs until you are certain no one knows who has whose snowball.

Then do the following:

- Post the numbers 1, 2, and 3 (or 1, 2, 3, 4, and 5, depending on the scale you use) on the wall in a space large enough for students to line up in front of them.

- Have students uncrumple their snowballs and line up in front of the number that matches what their snowball has for learning target 1. Count the number of students in each line. (You can graph this, if you like.) Read the learning target out loud.

- Repeat the process for each remaining learning target.

At the end of the activity, you will have a good idea of which learning targets need the most attention. You can then conduct a whole-class review focused on the greatest needs as identified by the human bar graph. Alternatively, you can use one of the followup options in the preceding activity.

During: Self-assessment While Completing an Assignment, Quiz, or Test

While students are completing any assignment that includes multiple-choice or short constructed response items, you can ask them to explain why they chose the answer they did. This gives them a chance to think more deeply about their answers and it gives you insight into misunderstandings and comprehension problems.

Format the assignment, quiz, or test so that after each selected response or fill-in item, students respond to the question, "How do you know your answer is correct?" as illustrated in Figure 4.8. When you review the assignment, quiz, or test with students, discuss common reasons for specific right and wrong choices. You can use their explanations diagnostically to determine which misconceptions to address in subsequent lessons. The information is especially useful when you will use the results of the assignment, quiz, or test formatively to guide your decisions about further instruction or to guide students in setting goals for their own learning needs.

Figure 4.8

FOR EXAMPLE

How Do You Know Your Answer Is Correct?

This reading comprehension question is designed to test students' ability to infer author's purpose.

Which of the following BEST sums up the author's purpose in writing this article?

a. To explain how the sliding rocks moved.

b. To explain how scientists determined how the rocks moved.

c. To explain how to conduct your own experiments.

d. To explain why the lake bed is called the Racetrack.

How do you know your answer is correct? _____

_____

Second-grade teacher Amy Meyer formats the assignment so that each problem begins with a statement of the learning target and has a box in the left margin next to it. While students are completing each problem, they assess their level of understanding by putting one of two symbols in the box: a star for "I think I know this" or stair steps for "I need more practice with this." Figure 4.9 shows an example of one student's work (Amy Meyer, Olentangy Local School District, Lewis Center, OH, personal communication, 2008).

Figure 4.9

FOR EXAMPLE

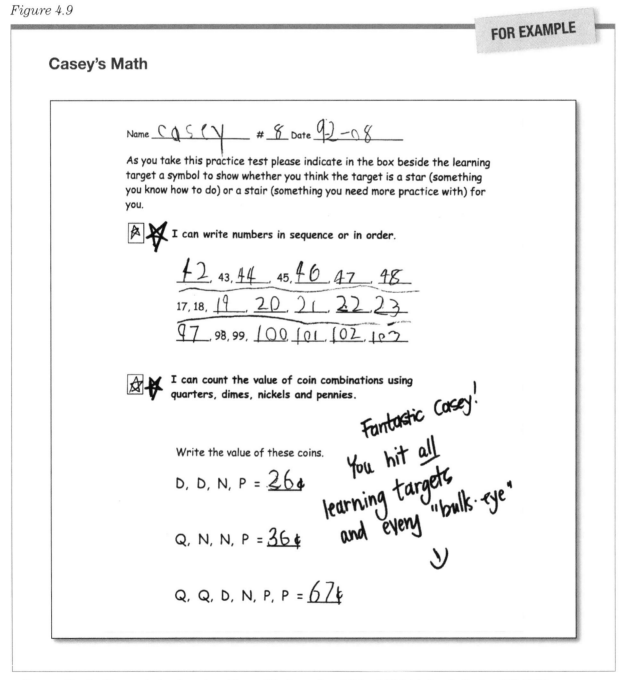

Casey's Math

Source: Used with permission from Amy Meyer, Olentangy Local School District, Lewis Center, OH, 2008.

After: Self-assessment and Goal Setting Using the Results of a Formative Quiz or Test

Students can use quiz or test results to identify which learning targets they have mastered and which ones they still need to work on. Students often take quizzes and tests without knowing what they measure beyond the most general level: "reading"; "social studies"; "science." If called on to use test results to set goals, without more specific understanding of what learning the test represents, students write the most general of goals: "study more"; "take my book home"; "try harder." Although noble, these goals don't focus on what students actually need to learn, and therefore are of limited use.

 Discrete Targets, Not Content Standards

Make sure the learning goal statements students are responding to are written as discrete learning targets and not as global complex content standards.

In this activity, you structure a test so that students can use the results to figure out what to do to improve their achievement. This, of course, works best on a formative assessment, that is, if there is a later opportunity to demonstrate achievement that counts for the mark or grade. The activity has two versions, one for elementary and one for secondary students. We'll look at the elementary version first and then discuss secondary modifications. Here is the process:

1. Identify which learning target each item on the quiz or test represents and fill out the first two columns of the form "Reviewing My Results" (Figure 4.10).

2. Administer the test or quiz, correct it, and hand it back to students, along with the form, "Reviewing My Results."

3. Students review their corrected tests or quizzes and mark the appropriate column—"Right" or "Wrong"—for each item.

4. Students mark the last two columns—"Simple Mistake" or "Don't Get It"—by reviewing the items they got wrong and asking themselves, "Do I know what I did wrong? Could I correct this myself?" If the answer is "Yes," they mark the "Simple Mistake" column. If the answer is "No," they mark the "Don't Get It" column. Now they have the raw material for determining their strengths and areas of greatest need.

5. Hand out the form, "Analyzing My Results" (Figure 4.11) and have students transfer each learning target to one (or more) of three categories: "I am good at these"; "I am pretty good at these, but need to do a little review"; and "I need to keep learning these."

6.   Last, students make a plan to improve. Figure 4.12 offers two examples of goal-setting frames you might have them use.

Before conducting this activity for the first time, you might want to show them the forms. Tell them that they are going to be using the results of this test or quiz to discover what they are good at and what they still need to learn. Ask in advance what kinds of simple mistakes they might make and what they might do to keep them from happening on this quiz or test.

Then, after they have taken the quiz or test, when they are analyzing their results, ask them to think about strategies for avoiding any simple mistakes they might have made and to write down what they believe will work for them.

Figure 4.10

Reviewing My Results

Name: _____   Assignment: _____   Date: _____

Please look at your corrected test and mark whether each problem is right or wrong. Then look at the problems you got wrong and decide if you made a simple mistake. If you did, mark the "Simple Mistake" column. For all the remaining problems you got wrong, mark the "Don't Get It" column.

Problem	Learning Target	Right	Wrong	Simple Mistake	Don't Get It
1					
2					
3					
4					
5					
6					
7					
8					
9					
10					

Figure 4.11

Analyzing My Results

I AM GOOD AT THESE!

Learning targets I got right:

I AM PRETTY GOOD AT THESE, BUT NEED TO DO A LITTLE REVIEW

Learning targets I got wrong because of a simple mistake:

What I can do to keep this from happening again:

I NEED TO KEEP LEARNING THESE

Learning targets I got wrong and I'm not sure what to do to correct them:

What I can do to get better at them:

Be prepared to offer suggestions for what students can do to get better as they are listing their "Don't Get It" targets. You might want to conduct one or more small-group reviews focused on specific learning targets for students who have identified those targets as areas of need. Or, offer suggestions for each learning target. ("To get better at learning target number 1, reread pages 246 to 250 and do problems 1 and 2 on page 251.")

Secondary Applications

If you work with secondary students, you may wish to make two modifications to the preceding activity. First, you may want them to track their level of confidence for each item as they take the quiz or test. And second, if they are referring to the form while they are taking the test, you may *not* want them to know which learning target each item is testing, because in some cases, that information will offer a clue to the correct answer.

Figure 4.12

Goal-setting Frames

To get better at _____ , I could. . .

One thing I am going to start doing is. . .

I'll start doing this on _____ and work on it until _____
                          date   *date*

One way I'll know I'm getting better is. . .

Goal	Steps	Evidence
What do I need to get better at?	How do I plan to do this?	What evidence will show I've achieved my goal?

Time Frame: Begin _____   End _____

Date _____   Signed _____

Source: Reprinted with permission from K. Gregory, C. Cameron, and A. Davies, *Knowing What Counts: Self-assessment and Goal-setting* (Merville, BC: Connections, 2000), p. 45.

Figure 4.13 shows an example of the form you could use. Instead of writing the learning target itself on the form, you make a separate numbered list and only write the number of the learning target next to each item number. While taking the test, students mark one of the two columns—confident or unsure—for each item after they have answered it. When you hand back the corrected tests, distribute the numbered list of learning targets and have students mark the rest of the columns on the form. Then on the second page of the form they categorize the learning targets as strengths, highest priorities for study, or in need of review.

Figure 4.13

Reviewing and Analyzing Results, Secondary Version

Name: _____　　Assignment: _____　　Date: _____

As you answer each question, decide whether you feel confident in your answer or are unsure about it and mark the corresponding box.

Problem #	Learning Target #	Confident	Unsure		Right	Wrong	Simple Mistake	Don't Get It
1								
2								
3								
4								
5								
6								
7								
8								
9								
10								
11								
12								
13								
14								
15								
16								

ANALYZING MY RESULTS

1. After your test has been corrected, identify which problems you got right and which you got wrong by putting Xs in the "Right" and "Wrong" columns.

2. Of the problems you got wrong, decide which ones were due to simple mistakes and mark the "Simple Mistake" column. (If it was a simple mistake, you can correct it without help.)

3. For all of the remaining wrong answers, mark the "Don't Get It" column.

Figure 4.13 (continued)

Name: _____   Assignment: _____   Date: _____

My Strengths

To identify your areas of strength, write down the learning targets for problems you felt confident about **and** got right.

Learning Target #	Learning Target or Problem Description

My Highest Priority for Studying

To determine what you need to study most, write down the learning targets for problems you marked "Don't Get It" (problems you got wrong, NOT because of a simple mistake).

Learning Target #	Learning Target or Problem Description

What I Need to Review

To determine what you need to review, write down the learning targets for problems you were unsure of and for problems on which you made simple mistakes.

Learning Target #	Learning Target or Problem Description

Source: Adapted with permission from S. Chappuis, R. Stiggins, J. Arter, and J. Chappuis, *Assessment* FOR *Learning: An Action Guide for School Leaders* (Portland, OR: Educational Testing Service, 2004), pp. 198, 199.

Students can develop an action plan to improve their understanding of the learning targets not yet mastered by completing a study plan, such as one of the goal-setting frames in Figure 4.12. As with elementary students, you might want to conduct one or more large- or small-group reviews focused on specific learning targets and offer study suggestions for each learning target. Alternatively, students can assign themselves to study groups based on their greatest needs; in this case, offer suggested activities for each group, to be conducted either in or outside of class.

If you are using this process with an end-of-unit test, students can submit the study plan as their ticket to a retake and take a parallel form of the test (same learning targets, different items) a few days later with the new score replacing the previous one.

Self-assessment and Goal Setting with Performance Assessment Rubrics

As you'll recall, White and Frederiksen (1998) noted significant learning gains from a combination of peer- and self-assessment with a rubric. The following strategies are designed for use when students are working on reasoning, performance skill, or product targets and demonstrating their achievement via performance assessment tasks evaluated by scoring rubrics. These practices guide them into using terms that describe specific features of quality when self-assessing.

Prerequisites

There are a number of ways to make self-assessing with a rubric work well for students, but there are prerequisites regarding rubric structure and students' experience with the rubric. The requirements that rubrics must fulfill are described in Chapter 2 and shown here in Figure 4.14. Preconditions for students include having practiced using the rubric to evaluate anonymous samples (Strategy 2) and having received feedback based on the rubric (Strategy 3). These prerequisites are important because the effectiveness of self-assessing and goal setting with a rubric hinges both on its content and on students' familiarity with it.

Figure 4.14

Features of Rubrics Suited for Self-assessment

Not all rubrics can be used well for self-assessment purposes. Those that are well suited to this purpose have the following features:

- They are general, rather than task specific.

- They use descriptive language that helps students see what they are doing right as well as what needs work.

- They are analytic rather than holistic in structure, if they are intended to address a complex or multidimensional learning target.

Ways to Format Rubric Text

You can take phrases from the rubric and insert them into a diagram or drawing to make the meaning stand out. For example, with younger students, where developmental continua phrases are suited to self-assessment, you can write selected phrases on the "Stars and Stairs" form (Figure 4.15), under the labels, "Just beginning," "On my way," and "Success." Students can use the form to document progress on individual learning targets represented in the rubric by identifying what in their work matches the step they think they're on.

As a class, you and your students can convert a rubric into a checklist of descriptive phrases for them to use to look over their work in advance of turning it in. Make sure the phrases on the checklist describe important elements of quality. Figure 4.16 shows an example of a writing checklist for elementary students, derived from the "6+1 Trait™ Writing Assessment Scoring Guide."

You can also plot the phrases from your rubric on a diagram, such as the target in Figure 4.17. Students can mark or highlight the level that best describes the quality of their work. You may also ask them to write a short statement of what they will do to move to the top level.

Or, students can mark which ring they think their current work sample hits. They can continue to mark and date the same form throughout the period of time devoted to mastering the target. (See Appendix B for blank target templates.)

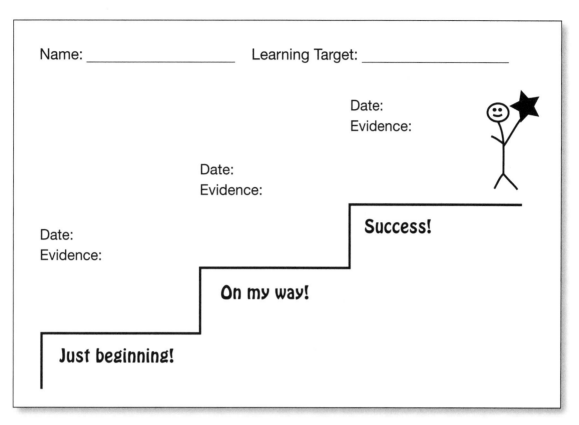

Stars and Stairs with Evidence

Name: _____   Learning Target: _____

Date:
Evidence:

Date:
Evidence:

Date:
Evidence:

Success!

On my way!

Just beginning!

Using the Rubric Itself

Students can mark phrases on the rubric describing strengths and problems they believe are present in their work. To distinguish between them, they can highlight the strengths in one color, such as green, and the problems in another, such as red. Have them also highlight their work to show which features correspond to the strengths and problems they highlighted on the rubric. Then, allow them time to revise their performance or product before submitting it for a mark or grade.

Alternatively, students can write the rubric phrase they believe describes a characteristic of their work, followed by a short description of the feature in their work that supports their judgment. In the example in Figure 4.18, a high school student has decided his essay's thesis statement is strong and has copied phrases from a rubric for social studies essays that he believes describe the statement. His next step is to write down the phrases in his thesis statement that illustrate each feature of quality he is claiming is present.

Figure 4.16

Self-check for a Story

Ideas and Content

_____ Is my message clear?

_____ Did I stick to one topic?

_____ Did I include details that are interesting and important?

Organization

_____ Does my story have an inviting introduction?

_____ Did I tell things in the best order?

_____ Does my story have a satisfying ending?

Voice

_____ Does this writing sound like me?

_____ Did I say what I think and feel?

_____ Can the reader tell I am interested in my story?

Word Choice

_____ Did I use words I love?

_____ Do my words make sense?

_____ Did I try not to repeat words too many times?

_____ Do my words paint a clear picture?

Sentence Fluency

_____ Are my sentences easy to read out loud?

_____ Do my sentences begin in different ways?

_____ Are some sentences long and some short?

Conventions

_____ Did I show where each paragraph starts?

_____ Did I look up the spelling of words I am not sure of?

_____ Did I use capital letters in the right places?

_____ Did I punctuate dialogue correctly?

_____ Did I use end punctuation (periods, exclamation marks, question marks) correctly?

Figure 4.17

Rubric Phrases Written on a Target

Writing a good introduction...

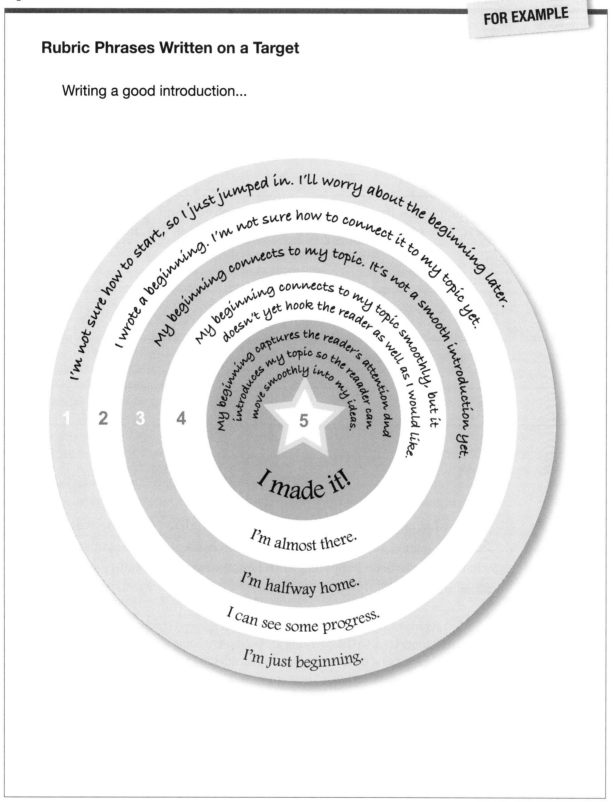

Figure 4.18

FOR EXAMPLE

Self-assessment with Rationale

Name: *Brad Smith*   **Date:** *Nov. 20*

Criterion: *Clear, analytical, and comprehensive thesis*

My rating: *Strong*

Rubric phrase that describes my work	Feature of my work that illustrates the phrase
Focuses on one specific aspect of the subject	
Makes an assertion that can be argued	
Covers only what I will address in my essay	

Teacher Laura Grayson has her second-grade students complete writing exit tickets (Figure 4.19) to develop the skill and habit of self-assessment. Here is what she has noticed happening with her students as a result (personal communication, 2008):

> The prompting questions on the exit ticket allowed students the opportunity to go back to their writing and complete some self-assessment prior to their writing conference with me. Students came to their conferences with an understanding of how they used the particular part of speech in their writing as well as a personal evaluation of whether it helped make the piece stronger. Students became aware of nuances in their own writing, such as a strong or weak lead, that in the past I had to point out to them. Students were making adjustments in their own writing and were eager to share how they had improved it.

Figure 4.19

Writing Exit Ticket

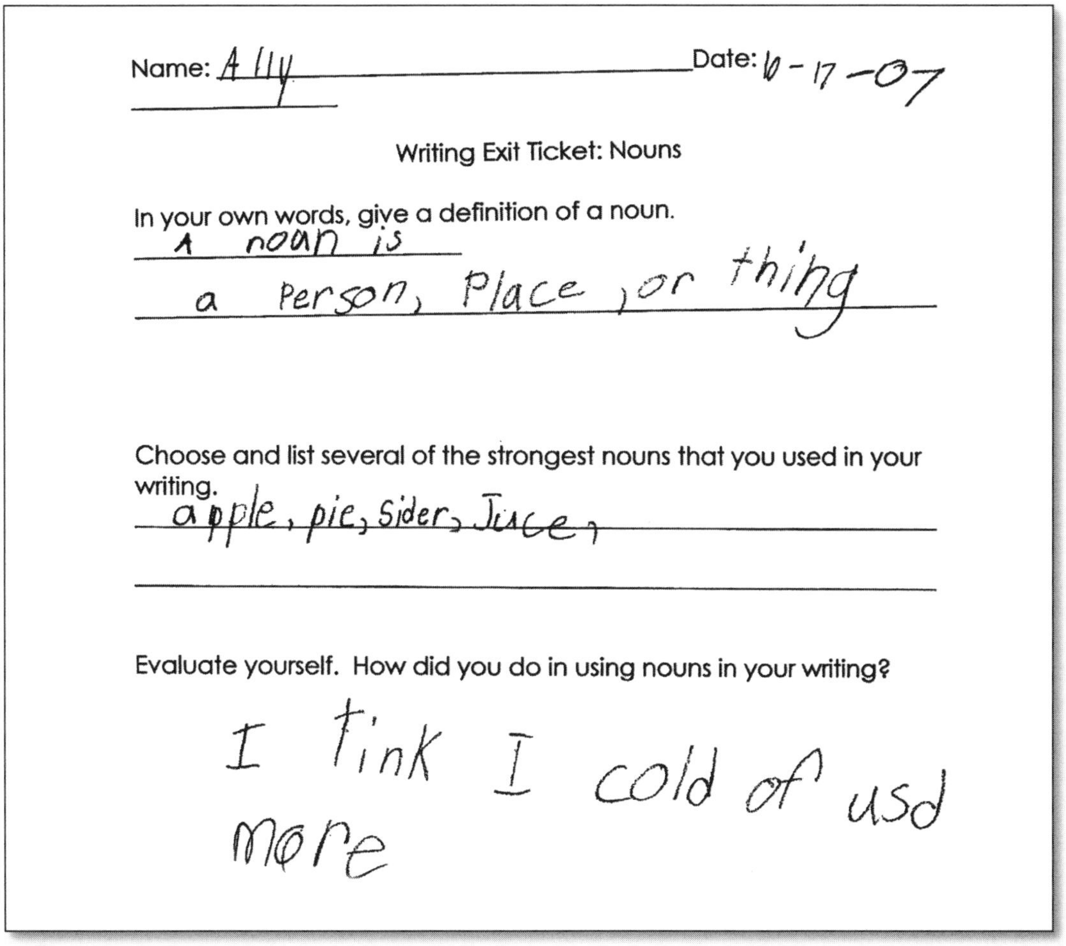

Name: _A lly_____ Date: _10 - 17 -07_

Writing Exit Ticket: Nouns

In your own words, give a definition of a noun.
A noun is
a person, place, or thing

Choose and list several of the strongest nouns that you used in your writing.
apple, pie, sider, Juce,

Evaluate yourself. How did you do in using nouns in your writing?
I tink I cold of usd more

Source: Used with permission from Laura Grayson, Mehlville School District, St. Louis, MO, 2008.

Goal Setting

Students don't always need to continue beyond the point of self-assessment—for instance, when there won't be further opportunities to continue studying these particular learning targets, or after achieving mastery. It makes sense in most other cases to ask students to consider what they could do to improve. They can base their goals on feedback from you, from a peer, on self-assessed areas of need, or on some combination of these sources of information.

Helping Students Set Specific, Challenging Goals

Goals that have the greatest impact on performance are what are called *hard goals*: specific rather than vague, and challenging rather than easy. Hard goals require students to move beyond their current level of achievement in some significant way (Sadler 1989). Goals that are specific identify the intended learning, describe the current status, and outline a plan of action. The plan can include a description of what the student will do, determination of assistance (if any) needed, a time frame, and identification of what evidence the student will use to verify accomplishment (Figure 4.20). The age of your students and the complexity of the learning will guide what you ask students to include in their action plans. In this case as in so many others, more is not always better; sometimes it's just more. To help students with the "challenging" part of the goal requirement, make sure they are selecting learning targets at their challenge level—difficult but within reach with effort.

"Hard goals work to focus attention, mobilize effort, and increase persistence at a task. By contrast, do-one's-best goals often turn out to be not much more effective than no goals at all."

Sadler, 1989, p. 129

Figure 4.20

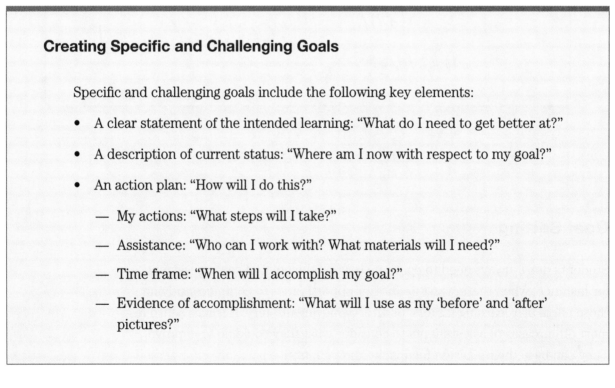

Creating Specific and Challenging Goals

Specific and challenging goals include the following key elements:

- A clear statement of the intended learning: "What do I need to get better at?"

- A description of current status: "Where am I now with respect to my goal?"

- An action plan: "How will I do this?"

  — My actions: "What steps will I take?"

  — Assistance: "Who can I work with? What materials will I need?"

  — Time frame: "When will I accomplish my goal?"

  — Evidence of accomplishment: "What will I use as my 'before' and 'after' pictures?"

For some learning targets, you can use a framework such as "Status, Target, Plan" to guide goal setting. It asks students to begin with *status*—a statement of where they are right now, followed by *target*—a statement of where they're headed, and last, *plan*—a description of how they'll get there. Figure 4.21 illustrates this with a physical education goal.

Figure 4.22 shows an example of a high school student's health goal and plan. In Appendix B you will find frames that illustrate various ways to elicit specificity from students. You may need to model how to fill out a planning frame so students can see how to set long-term goals. Some students may also need individual help in completing a frame. (See Appendix B for reproducible forms of all the goal-setting frames in this chapter, as well as a collection of blank forms for short self-assessment and goal-setting activities.)

Figure 4.21

FOR EXAMPLE

Status, Target, Plan

Status: Right now I can ___do 2 pushups___

Target: My goal is to ___do 10 pushups___ by ___2 weeks___

Plan: To reach my goal I will ___do 2 pushups morning & night for 2 days. Then 2 sets of 3 pushups morning & night for 2 days. Then 2 sets of 4 pushups morning & night for 2 days. Then 2 sets of 6 pushups morning & night for 2 days. Last 2 sets of 8 pushups morning & night for 2 days.___

I will get help from ___me myself and I___

Figure 4.22

Eleventh-Grade Student's Health Goal and Plan

Name: *John Jurjevich*	Date: *Feb. 20, 2009*

What I need to learn:

I will learn to diagram how the immune system works.

Evidence of current level of achievement:

Test on communicable diseases 2/18/09

Plan of action:

I will study the pages on pathogens and the immune system in the book and will practice creating a picture of how the immune system works, with all parts labeled.

Help needed—what and who:

My book and me

Time frame:

I will be ready to be re-tested on Feb. 26

Evidence of achieving my goal:

Test on Feb. 26

Source: Adapted with permission from R. Stiggins, J. Arter., J. Chappuis, and S. Chappuis., *Classroom Assessment* for *Student Learning: Doing It Right—Using It Well* (Portland, OR: Educational Testing Service, 2004), p. 369.

The Goal-setting Conference

You may want to meet with a few students individually or in small groups to help them work through setting their goals.

1.   Begin by sharing the intended learning in terms they understand. ("Here's what we're working on being able to do.")

2.   Next, look together at work they have produced to determine what they already know. Guide them in the formulation of a goal statement regarding what they need to learn.

3. Ask them to describe how they might go about accomplishing their goal. Help them identify reasonable actions likely to result in maximum learning, if needed. Have them write down the actions they will take.

4. Help them determine whether they will need or want assistance from another person and what materials, if any, they will need.

5. Set a time frame or ask them to.

6. Help them identify what artifact(s) they will use as evidence of *meeting* their goal.

Your students can also work with partners to help each other set goals.

Conclusion

Meaningful student self-assessment and goal setting require clear targets to begin with. Beyond that, students need to be taught to compare their status to the targets, justify their judgments with evidence from their work, and set specific goals that guide subsequent actions.

When we teach students to self-assess with these conditions in place, they can do it accurately. Indeed, they are often harder on themselves than you would be. If you think back through the activities in this chapter, you'll notice that students are giving you a gold mine of information about what they know and what they need, assessment *for* learning data that you did not have to create an extra assignment, task, quiz, or test to obtain. You can use the information to group students, to assign partners, to reteach, to dig deeper into understanding, and to enrich students' learning.

CHAPTER 5

How Can I Close the Gap?
Focused Teaching and Revision

Strategy 5

Design lessons to focus on one learning target or aspect
of quality at a time.

Strategy 6

Teach students focused revision.

Strategy 5
Design lessons to focus on one learning target or aspect of quality at a time.

Strategy 6
Teach students focused revision.

Sadler (1989) identified that, in order for improvement to take place, the child must first know the purpose of the task, then how far this was achieved, and finally be given help in knowing how to move closer towards the desired goal or 'in closing the gap'. It is perhaps the last aspect that we have not always helped children to maximize their achievement.

—*Clarke, 1998, p. 68*

G ood formative assessment tells us where students are now in their learning. Strategies 5 and 6 use that information as a starting block. Strategy 5 targets instruction to the learning gaps—incomplete understanding, misconceptions, partially developed skills, and the like, while Strategy 6 engages students in focused revision—practice, with feedback—during the lessons delivered in Strategy 5. They work in tandem: focused instruction followed by focused practice.

There are as many ways to target instruction as there are learning targets in your curriculum. This chapter will offer examples of how you can extend assessment-related activities from Strategies 1 through 4 to offer students more instruction and practice with learning targets you have previously identified as needing further attention. The examples all illustrate ways of creating short practice assignments to make the learning more manageable, especially for struggling students who may be facing multiple gaps in need of bridging. Short, focused tasks "scaffold" the learn-

"[A]ssessment insights must be used immediately as part of the instructional process. . . . Formative assessment is effective, then, when it is timed so that the information can be used . . ."

Shepard, 2008, p. 294

ing—they remove some of the complexities at first, so students can pay attention to key concepts, strategies, or skills. We will first look at scaffolding ideas you can use with selected response and short constructed response items, then at ideas for use with performance assessment tasks and rubrics.

Scaffolding with Selected Response and Short Constructed Response Items

We can use selected response items and short constructed response items to measure knowledge and reasoning learning targets; those items can be used to move students towards mastery, too. The following activities show how selected response and short answer methodology can address problems related to content knowledge and development of reasoning proficiencies.

Identifying and Using Typical Misconceptions and Reasoning Errors

Strategy 5 suggests that you select or design lessons to teach students how to recognize and avoid the particular problems they predictably demonstrate. Often you can get good information about students' problems by paying attention to their wrong answers—by listening to their explanations and analyzing problems evident within their work. Discussions with colleagues can also uncover reasoning errors, instances of partial understanding, and outright misconceptions that students often have. The operative question here is "When students go sideways on this learning target, what are the typical problems?"

"I hate those questions where they don't tell you the answers!"

Mary Shannon, age 11

One simple approach is to list these problems and as you teach to rectify them, periodically ask students to mark, date, and explain those they can now correct (Figure 5.1). Or, you might make a list of major conceptual understandings you will address in a given unit, mixing in statements reflecting misconceptions students typically have. Ask students to mark "True," "False," or "Unsure" next to each one. Periodically, hand out a fresh copy of the list and have students revisit the statements related to what you have taught to that point, marking the statements as either true or false, accompanied by an explanation: "I think it is true/false because _____." Figure 5.2 shows a variation of this activity with a seventh-grade mathematics unit.

Figure 5.1

Correcting Misconceptions

Misconception	Date	Correction
1.		
2.		
3.		

Figure 5.2

FOR EXAMPLE

Buckle Down Lesson 10—Geometric Measurements

Name:_____   Period:_____   Date:_____

Before reading	Statement	After Reading
True False	Pi ≈ 3.14	True False
True False	Area is the measure of the inside of a two-dimensional figure.	True False
True False	Volume is measured in square units.	True False
True False	The formula to find the area of a triangle is ½ *bh*.	True False
True False	The area of a composite shape can be found by breaking the shape down into common shapes.	True False
True False	*B* represents a length measurement.	True False
True False	Volume is the amount of space a shape takes up.	True False
True False	The area of a circle is the same as the area of a sector.	True False

Source: Used with permission from Beth Cotsmire, Bucyrus City Schools, Bucyrus, OH, 2008.

Multiple-choice Items as Teaching Tools

Multiple-choice items can be used in formative assessment contexts if they are constructed so that the wrong answers (called "distractors") represent faulty reasoning, misconceptions, or partial understanding. When lots of students select the same incorrect answer, you can immediately see the common misconception or error and act to fix it. In addition, the wrong answers can act as "weak" examples that, in contrast with the correct answer, help students better understand the learning target.

When creating a multiple-choice item addressing a knowledge target, identifying helpful distractors is pretty straightforward: insert incorrect knowledge as the wrong answer choices. With continued experience in one content area and one age group, you will notice patterns of partial understanding *vis à vis* the knowledge to be mastered, which can be turned into distractors on practice tests. And, as students improve over time, the distractors will become less useful—a hoped-for obsolescence.

When creating multiple-choice items for patterns of reasoning, you can develop distractors by framing a multiple-choice question as a fill-in-the-blank question first. Examine students' wrong answers closely to determine typical errors or misconceptions. Then describe the characteristics of each typical error or misconception; these become your "distractor formulas." Also, write a description of the characteristics of the correct answer, which should parallel your student-friendly definition of the reasoning target.

Distractors

Multiple-choice distractors should all be plausible choices, each reflecting a misunderstanding or partial understanding of the learning target the item is intended to measure.

For example, if you want to create distractors for the reasoning target "Makes a generalization," you could ask students to read a short text explaining something such as how meat-eating plants function and then pose the following question: "What generalization can you make from this passage about how these plants lure their prey?" Upon examining student responses, you may find the following characteristics:

- The right answer is a statement that is true for the evidence presented and extends the application (generalizes) logically to a broader array of instances (*student-friendly definition*).

- Some wrong answers offer a statement that is true for the evidence presented, but the application (generalization) includes too broad an array of instances to be supported by evidence (*overgeneralization*).

- Some wrong answers offer a statement that is true for the evidence presented, but does not include an extension to other instances (*no generalization present*).

- Some wrong answers offer a statement that is not true for the evidence presented (*incorrect interpretation of evidence*).

Now you have a list of common errors in reasoning—distractor descriptions—for *generalization*. Figure 5.3 shows distractors for a sampling of reasoning targets that can be assessed with multiple-choice items.

Once you have written distractor descriptions, you can create a variety of practice lessons. In the inference example shown in Figure 5.4, all of the incorrect answers are guesses based on faulty interpretations of different sentences in the reading passage. To practice inferring, students can work with a partner to find an answer they know to be incorrect and explain why it is wrong. They then can share their choice and explanation with another pair of students. Or, students can work with a partner to select the correct answer and explain why it is correct. By justifying their judgments, students are building understanding of the learning target—in this case, of what makes a good inference.

 Creating Multiple-choice Items

Preparing materials for these activities requires knowing how to construct items accurately. See Stiggins et al., 2004, Chapter 5, for further guidance.

Figure 5.5 gives an elementary-level example of a focused lesson for the learning target "Makes an inference," in which students use the student-friendly definition (the right answer description) as well as the distractor descriptions to differentiate between the correct and incorrect answers.

Here is another process for using distractors as teaching tools:

1. Select a text passage and develop your own question and possible answers using your right-answer and distractor descriptions.

2. Give the question, the possible answers, and the descriptions to students.

3. Have students read the passage, and then match each answer choice to its description.

Figure 5.3

FOR EXAMPLE

Distractors for Selected Reasoning Targets

1. Infer

Question: What idea could you infer from the text? Or, Which idea does this selection suggest?

Possible Answers:
- The right answer—a guess based on clues you can find in the text
- A wrong answer—a guess that seems reasonable, but that evidence in the text does not support
- A wrong answer—not even a guess, just information recopied from the text

2. Summarize

Question: What sentence best summarizes what this (selection) is about?

Possible Answers:
- The right answer—a brief statement of the main points or ideas
- A wrong answer—a statement including an idea not found in the passage
- A wrong answer—a statement including an idea from the passage that is too narrow to be acceptable as a summary

3. Compare and Contrast

Question: Which sentence tells how _____ (two or more items) are alike? Or, Which sentence tells how _____ (two or more items) differ?

Possible Answers:
- The right answer—a statement of an appropriate similarity
- A wrong answer—a statement that is true of one of the items to be compared, but not true of the other

  Or

- The right answer—a statement of an appropriate difference
- A wrong answer—a statement that claims an inaccurate difference

4. Identify Cause and Effect

Question: Which sentence explains why _____(event) happened?

Possible Answers:
- The right answer—a reasonable statement of causation
- A wrong answer—a statement of causation that a careful reading of the text does not support

Source: Adapted with permission from *Washington Assessment of Student Learning 4th Grade Reading Test and Item Specifications* (Olympia, WA: Office of Superintendent of Public Instruction, 1998), n.p.

Figure 5.4

Assessment *for* Learning with an Inference Item

Directions to Students:

The following passage is taken from the book *Down the Great Unknown* by Edward Dolnick, an account of an 1869 exploration of the Colorado River.

Read the paragraph and then read the test question.

> [T]he men were confident about the expedition, the mood a happy mix of can-do optimism and "school's out for summer" boisterousness after the dreary weeks at Green River Station. Ignorance was not quite bliss, but it veered in that direction. Powell, for one, took for granted that outdoor expertise in general would translate into river experience in particular. "The hunters managed the pack train last year, and will largely man the boats this," he wrote matter-of-factly. The tone implied that the switch from horses and mules to boats was trifling, akin perhaps to a switch from guitar to banjo.

Which of the following ideas does this passage suggest about the men of the expedition?

    a) They were not educated.

    b) They did not have experience navigating rivers.

    c) They had just gotten out of school for the summer.

    d) They were going to learn to play the banjo.

Select one of the answers you think is incorrect and explain why you think it is wrong.

Incorrect answer: _____

Why: _____

_____

_____

_____

Figure 5.5

Why Is This Wrong?

Which **one** of these answers is a good inference, based on the passage from *Danny the Champion of the World* that you just read? Mark the good inference with a star. The right answer is a good inference because it is a **guess based on clues,** or evidence, from the story.

    a. The BFG could hear extremely well because he could not see very well.

    b. The author loved his father very much.

    c. The father did not finish high school.

    d. The father had a good imagination.

    e. The father wanted people to think he was a serious man.

    f. The father had a well-developed sense of hearing.

    g. The father was a funny person.

Some of these answers are wrong because they are **not inferences at all.** They are just facts that the story tells you outright. Write the letters of those wrong answers here:

_____.

Some of the answers are wrong because, even though they are guesses, **the evidence in the story does not support them.** Write the letters of those wrong answers here:

_____.

Source: Adapted with permission from R. Stiggins, J. Arter, J. Chappuis, and S. Chappuis, *Classroom Assessment* for *Student Learning: Doing It Right—Using It Well* (Portland, OR: Educational Testing Service, 2004), p. 154.

Figure 5.6 illustrates this matching activity with right-answer and distractor descriptions for *generalization.*

These practice exercises help students realize wrong answer choices are wrong for a reason—it's not actually "mystical choice"—and reinforce why the right answer is right.

Figure 5.6

Matching Answer Choices to Right-answer and Distractor Descriptions

(Students read text about a scientific investigation in Death Valley.) *Which statement can you support after reading this selection?* One of these statements is a defensible generalization and the other three are not. Draw a line between each possible answer and the statement that describes it.

Possible Answer	Description
a. Crazy-sounding theories can be ruled out before designing an experiment.	w. Right—True for the evidence presented and extends the application logically to a broader array of instances
b. Sharp and Carey proved to the world that the rocks moved on their own.	x. Wrong—True for the evidence presented, but the statement includes too broad an array of instances to be supported by evidence
c. Death Valley is a place where things happen without explanation.	y. Wrong—True for the evidence presented, but does not include an extension to other instances
d. Questions about the world around us can be answered through scientific investigation.	z. Wrong—Not true for the evidence presented

Using Graphic Organizers as Teaching Tools

If you have used activities such as those described in Strategies 1 and 2 to define a reasoning learning target, students can practice applying that definition by using a graphic organizer (a visual cue to the elements of quality for that particular pattern of reasoning). For example, Figure 5.7 shows a graphic organizer students can use to practice answering selected response or short answer items calling for a generalization.

Graphic Organizers for Patterns of Reasoning

For maximum learning, the graphic organizer you choose should be a visual representation of the definition of the learning target you have shared with students.

To use a graphic organizer as a teaching tool, first, find or create a good question to test the pattern of reasoning you are focusing on. Have students read the text the question refers to, and then work through completing the graphic organizer with them as a large group. Next, ask them to read one or more additional passages and answer questions aimed at the pattern of reasoning by completing the graphic organizer. Students can do this initially with a partner and then individually. (See Appendix B for more examples of graphic organizers for different patterns of reasoning.)

Figure 5.7

FOR EXAMPLE

Graphic Organizer for Making a Generalization

When we make a generalization, we compare the pieces of evidence at hand to see what they have in common. Then we make a statement that is true for the pieces of evidence at hand and is also true for a broader array of instances. A generalization is an example of inductive inference.

Write the commonalities in the outer circles, then make a statement that would apply to the specific examples and also to others like them.

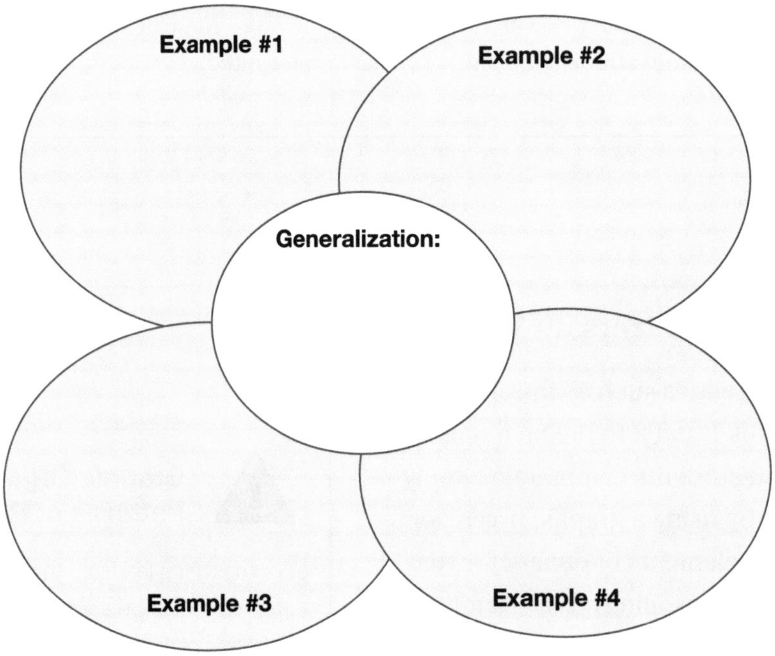

Example #1

Example #2

Generalization:

Example #3

Example #4

Scaffolding with Performance Assessment Tasks and Rubrics

The following activities are appropriate when students need further practice with those reasoning, performance skill, and product targets most appropriately assessed with a performance task and rubric. In these instances, you create practice lessons by narrowing the focus of the task and/or the rubric.

Creating Focused Tasks

If your ultimate learning target calls for completion of a complex task (such as solving a multistep mathematics problem, writing a research paper, conducting a science investigation, or writing an analysis of primary source documents), you can design practice around aspects of the task that you know will be difficult for some or all students. The following examples illustrate focused tasks in mathematics, writing, and science.

In mathematics, when your students are unsure of how to choose a strategy to solve a problem, you can use a series of short, focused problems to teach them how. Begin by demonstrating one problem-solving strategy (e.g., drawing a picture) with a problem suited to it, then give students a few other problems to solve using the strategy you demonstrated. Ask them to share their work with a small group and together come up with an answer to the question, "What does this strategy help us do?" Demonstrate a second problem-solving strategy (e.g., make a tree diagram) with a different problem and repeat the process. Next, give them a new problem (one that could be solved with one or both of the strategies they have practiced) and ask them to choose which of the two strategies to use. You can have them work in pairs to make the decision and write an explanation of why they chose that strategy, then compare their thinking with another pair, before conducting a large-group discussion of what each strategy is best suited for and when you might use it. Figure 5.8 shows a list of problem-solving strategies that you could select from depending on what your mathematics problem-solving content standards call for.

In writing, if your students have difficulty getting started, you can model two or three ways to generate ideas, then give them a short focused writing task, asking them to choose one idea-generation strategy and practice using it with this task. Or, if they have difficulty narrowing a topic, you can prepare a list of topics, some of which are narrow enough to be addressed fully in the given time

Figure 5.8

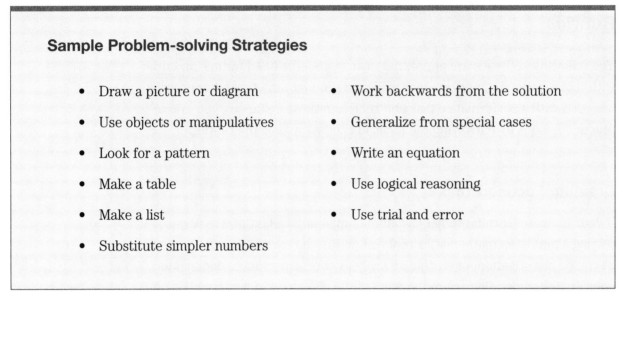

Sample Problem-solving Strategies

- Draw a picture or diagram
- Use objects or manipulatives
- Look for a pattern
- Make a table
- Make a list
- Substitute simpler numbers

- Work backwards from the solution
- Generalize from special cases
- Write an equation
- Use logical reasoning
- Use trial and error

and some of which are not, and have students work in pairs or small groups to discuss which topics fit each category and why. Next, you can select one of the broad topics and model how to narrow it. Finally, students can select a topic and rework it so that it is narrow enough to address in the given time.

In science, if students need work with preparing understandable data displays, you can first model options to use with different data sets. Next, give them new data sets and have them work in pairs to create a display that is suited to the data and is clearly understandable.

These examples relating to math, writing, and science illustrate a process useful in any discipline to identify one part of a complex task and teach to it specifically, engaging students in practice and discussion, before having them take on the full-blown assignment.

Common Formative Assessment Tasks

If you are a part of a team creating formative tasks to be used across classrooms, you can design them to focus on individual learning targets you have determined to be of greatest need.

Figure 5.9 is a letter accompanying "Task of the Month," a districtwide application of this idea for mathematics, reading, and writing at the elementary level. Mathematics tasks were drawn from published materials, accompanied by student samples of work at all levels of quality, aligned to state standards and assessments. For reading tasks, students read passages from district-adopted language arts and social studies texts and answered questions aimed at the same content standards tested by the state assessment. The writing tasks were created to elicit the kinds of writing expected at each grade level: narrative, informational, and persuasive. Teaching tips drawn from Strategies 1 through 7 accompanied each task. None was intended to be used solely as summative evaluation.

Figure 5.9

Task of the Month

Curriculum Department, Central Kitsap School District
Silverdale, Washington

January 27, 1998

TO: Grades 3, 4, and 5 Teachers

FROM: Gordon Bushaw, Jan Chappuis, and Shannon Thompson

RE: TASK OF THE MONTH

It's Task-of-the-Month time again! There's a lot of material here this month from which you can pick and choose.

There are three reading tasks for January. The main task, "Animal Lookalikes," can be used to teach and assess *comprehension and analysis of nonfictional text*. One supplementary task, "Table of Contents," measures *comprehension of nonfictional text* and the other, "The Lion and the Mouse," measures *comprehension of fictional text*. Specific learning targets for each task are shown on the attached matrix. We will continue to provide you with reading tasks each month that give your students experience with the range of learning targets they will encounter on the fourth grade Washington Assessment of Student Learning.

This month's mathematics task, "Odd Wins," addresses probability. It can be used as a teaching tool and/or a test of students' ability to solve a probability problem. We encourage you to assess their responses for problem solving and for communication.

Figure 5.9 (continued)

Please do not be worried about how much "stuff" is here for mathematics; go through it and decide what suits your students' and your own needs best. The following supporting materials are included:

- General guidelines for using a mathematics task as a teaching tool
- Tips for teaching probability using "Odd Wins"
- Two forms to choose from if your students need some help planning a strategy and drafting an explanation
- A chart of problem-solving strategies
- Student self-checklists for problem solving and communication
- Mathematics problem solving bookmarks
- Three versions of the mathematics scoring guide for problem solving and communication—one suited for grades 3–4, one for grades 5–6, and one for you.

In addition, the second mathematics task, "Hot Dogs," could be used if you want to give students more practice with communicating mathematically.

The writing task for January, "Amazing Animal Tales," requires students to write a *fictional narrative*. We have included a short definition of a fictional narrative and a description of the components present in a good one. If you haven't taught students the form of this genre, your language text, *World of Language*, has some helpful advice. We encourage you to evaluate "Amazing Animal Tales" for the traits of *Ideas*, *Organization*, and *Conventions*. A student self-check with these three traits is also included. You could run it on the back of the task so students would have it available as they revise.

Through January's material, you will find references to using these tasks as a teaching tool. Analyses of research clearly indicate that one of the most powerful strategies for improving student performance is to give them the criteria by which their work will be judged—*in advance, and in words they can understand*. When students use the criteria while planning and revising their work, quality improves.

When you use a task as a teaching tool, you are using it to go deeper into one aspect of good performance, slowing down the completion of the task to have students self-assess with criteria they understand. You may even be slowing down in the middle of the task to teach the criteria, by sharing anonymous samples of strong and weak performance on a similar, but not identical, task, and having students evaluate them, before completing the task of the month. You may be stopping in the middle, deliberately, to teach a mini-lesson on one skill needed (how to write a good introduction, for example). These suggestions this month give you opportunities to do this—to use assessment as instruction.

Feel free to call or email us with any questions, comments, or suggestions. We appreciate your feedback.

Source: Adapted with permission from Central Kitsap School District, Silverdale, WA, 1998.

Practicing One Criterion at a Time

When you are planning to evaluate students' final products or performances with a scoring rubric, you can move directly from Strategy 2 activities into Strategy 5 and 6 activities for practice. The following suggestions work best after students have had experience using the rubric to differentiate between strong and weak samples.

1. Students work with partners to revise a previously scored weak sample. They focus on one criterion from the scoring rubric and use its phrases to guide their revision. They can compare their new draft to that of another pair, then revise again, if needed. Or, they can decide which is the better revision and describe why. They can also use the rubric to score their final revision.

2. Share a sample of work from published sources (e.g., newspapers, magazines, pamphlets, government documents, videotaped footage) that falls in the mid to low range on one criterion of your scoring rubric. Let students evaluate the sample using the rubric, discuss its problems, and then revise it based on their observations about what it needs.

3. Students work with a partner to create a revision plan describing what the author of a previously evaluated anonymous sample can do to make it strong for the specified criterion or criteria. Or they write a letter to the author of the sample ("Dear Anonymous, . . ."), explaining what steps to take to improve it for one or more selected aspects of quality.

4. Students work individually or in pairs to revise their own work, using the scoring rubric to point the way to an exemplary product or performance.

5. Students write an explanation of what they can do to make their product or performance exemplary for the criterion they are focusing on. Or, they write themselves a revision letter ("Dear Me, . . .") detailing the steps they can take to improve their work. In an assessment *for* learning context, students do not necessarily need to execute their plans—the plans can function as evidence of whether they have as yet grasped the central concepts of quality, leading you either to continue focused teaching or to move on.

6. Another way to give students practice with selected criteria is to take a shot at developing the product or performance in front of your class. Don't be afraid to model the messy underside: students can benefit when you model using concepts from the scoring rubric to help you think your way through the problems you encounter. Let students use the scoring rubric concepts to give you suggestions along the way. This activity can also function as preparation for students to give peer feedback.

7. Let students share their process and reasoning by modeling them for the class.

Conclusion

Figure 5.10, an excerpt from a teacher's grading policy statement, is an example of where the focused teaching of Strategies 5 and 6 fits into the teaching/learning/assessing cycle in a high school mathematics class. When assessment raises awareness of learning gaps, Strategies 5 and 6 build the bridge between your students and the desired achievement. You can choose from or modify examples in this chapter to strengthen students' knowledge, reasoning, and performance capabilities prior to testing or performing for a summative score or grade.

Figure 5.10

Excerpt from a High School Mathematics Grading Policy

Assessment for Learning

In this course, our main focus is for each student to understand the concepts of Pre-Calculus and be able to apply them to solve problems. In order to best promote and support students' learning, we are going to shift our assessment practices so students will have a clear understanding of what they are expected to know and be able to do. Students will be given many opportunities to practice these skills and work to master the content through classroom activities, homework, and penalty-free quizzes before showing what they know on our summative tests. Students will frequently be asked to self-assess their understanding, and to work in pairs, small groups, or as a class to improve each others' comprehension.

Homework

Students will be given homework assignments to practice their skills individually on a regular basis. These assignments are crucial for students to expand their understanding, and will give both the students and me an opportunity to check their comprehension of small chunks of material before moving on. It is very important that the students attempt and give serious thought to all problems, as our difficult content is best learned through this individual practice and sometimes struggle. Homework assignments will be discussed and checked the next day in class, giving students the opportunity to ask questions of each other and me to further increase their understanding.

Formative Quizzes

We will have short, penalty-free quizzes about once a week throughout the year. The sole purpose of these quizzes is for students to gauge their current understanding and correct misconceptions. These quizzes will not count as a part of a student's grade, but will be used to determine which concepts each student needs to work with more to master. I will record scores to keep track of students' progress with the material as we move through a unit, and may use quiz scores to determine homework or to group students for appropriate class work to help each student improve understanding.

Summative Tests

At the end of each unit of material, we will have a test where students will be asked to show that they have learned the material, can perform necessary skills, and can apply concepts to solve problems. These tests will be the great majority of students' grades each quarter. Students can expect about three summative tests each quarter, and they will be able to retake any test to show later mastery.

Figure 5.10 (continued)

Projects/Class Assignments

There may be a few projects or other classroom assignments where students will be asked to apply previous knowledge to real-life tasks or in-depth problems. These assignments may be graded and count toward students' quarter grades.

Test Retake Policy

Each student has the option to retake each unit test once and will receive the higher score. If you want to retake a unit test you must meet these conditions:

—Have all homework from the unit complete.
—Complete test corrections from the original test.
—Turn in these corrections and your original test to me.
—Schedule a time to retake the test.

Source: Adapted with permission from Jeanette Kenney, unpublished classroom materials, Olentangy Local School District, Lewis Center, OH, 2008.

CHAPTER 6

How Can I Close the Gap?
Tracking, Reflecting on, and Sharing Learning

Strategy 7

Engage students in self-reflection, and let them keep track of and share their learning.

Strategy 7

Engage students in self-reflection, and let them keep track of and share their learning.

> [We] help our students become increasingly efficacious when we . . . help them learn how to improve the quality of their work one key attribute at a time, when we help them learn to see and keep track of changes in their own capabilities, and when we help them reflect on the relationships between those improvements and their own actions.
>
> —*Stiggins, 2007, p. 75*

*S*taying in touch with your own progress toward a goal and knowing when you have reached it both reinforce the value of effort. When students track progress, reflect on their learning processes and growth, and share observations about achievement or about themselves as learners, it helps anchor their learning in long-term memory. Strategy 7 is a gap-closing strategy because of its impact on student motivation and retention.

To implement these final activities successfully, students need a clear vision of where they are headed and where they are now, and they need to have made some gains along the way. Strategies 1 through 6 prepare students with the information and the progress required to answer the question implicit in Strategy 7: "What have I learned?" In this chapter, we'll examine ways to help students track their learning, reflect on it, and share it with others.

Students Keeping Track of Their Learning

Keeping track of learning can be motivating in and of itself, if while recording information students can see positive change. Having some record of achievement or collection of evidence is also a prerequisite for engaging in self-reflection activities and being able to discuss progress meaningfully with others. Students can track their learning in a variety of ways, which we will examine in three categories: recording progress, keeping learning journals, and collecting samples of work.

Recording Progress

Some of what you teach may lend itself to tracking progress assignment by assignment or learning target by learning target. For maximum effect, tracking forms should link each entry to a learning target and include a place for students to record and date their results on multiple trials, as illustrated in Figures 6.1 through 6.4. See Appendix B for reproducible versions of the forms referenced in this chapter.

The form in Figure 6.1 organizes assessment information by assignment and includes the following:

- The name of the assignment (e.g., page number, title, project name)

- The date turned in and identifying information for learning target(s) addressed (e.g., numbers transferred from a list of learning targets for the unit or marking period that you have handed out)

- The mark or score the assignment received (e.g., points earned/ points possible)

- Whether the assignment was formative (for practice) or summative (for a mark or grade)

- Space for students to record strengths (which they mark with a star symbol) and area(s) for improvement or next steps (which they mark with the stairs symbol)

Figure 6.1

Tracking Progress by Assignment

Assignment	Date	Target	Score	F/S	★ ⌐

Figure 6.2 shows an example with mathematics targets using the "Stars and Stairs" format, where students color in the star and record the date as they achieve the target on each step. You can use a form like this with any developmentally sequenced set of learning targets written in student-friendly language.

Figure 6.3 shows an example of students graphing their results on practice assignments and tests for a collection of reading learning targets. Here, two of the targets, "Identifies synonyms and antonyms" and "Understands the meaning of prefixes and suffixes," are knowledge targets most likely practiced and assessed with selected response questions. The third target, "Reads aloud with fluency," is a performance skill target evaluated with a five-point scoring rubric. This example demonstrates that students can graph their results with any combination of learning targets to help them see their progress assignment by assignment, or task by task.

Figure 6.4 shows an example set up for students to describe their strengths and areas for further work on multiple trials with social studies targets that call for an extended written response. With learning targets such as these, students can keep track of their progress by recording the feedback comments you have given and/or their own self-assessment observations.

Keeping Learning Journals

A student's learning journal is in essence a collection of thoughts about any aspect of learning—questions, insights, observations about things that are

Figure 6.2

Student Tracking Form: Fourth-grade Mathematics Targets

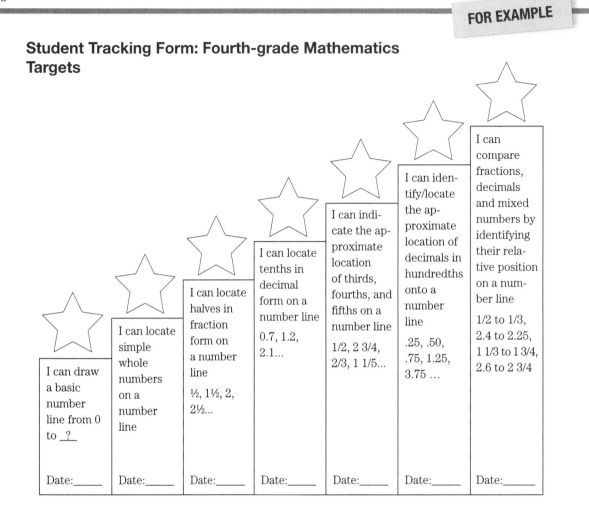

I can draw a basic number line from 0 to _?_

Date:_____

I can locate simple whole numbers on a number line

Date:_____

I can locate halves in fraction form on a number line

½, 1½, 2, 2½...

Date:_____

I can locate tenths in decimal form on a number line

0.7, 1.2, 2.1...

Date:_____

I can indicate the approximate location of thirds, fourths, and fifths on a number line

1/2, 2 3/4, 2/3, 1 1/5...

Date:_____

I can identify/locate the approximate location of decimals in hundredths onto a number line

.25, .50, .75, 1.25, 3.75 ...

Date:_____

I can compare fractions, decimals and mixed numbers by identifying their relative position on a number line

1/2 to 1/3, 2.4 to 2.25, 1 1/3 to 1 3/4, 2.6 to 2 3/4

Date:_____

Source: Adapted with permission from Rick Croom, unpublished classroom materials, San Juan Unified School District, Carmichael, CA, 2008.

important, likes and dislikes, progress, strengths, areas for improvement, and so forth. It can be purposefully comprehensive or idiosyncratic, elaborate in style or made from whatever is at hand. It can be kept electronically, recorded, or handwritten. Students can create their own journal books or they can use spiral-bound–type notebooks; even a manila folder will do. What makes it a learning journal is what students put into it.

Let's start with the simple manila folder. This is a learning journal in its "loose collection" form—a place to keep all of the feedback, self-assessment, and goal-setting forms students have received and completed, especially if finished

Figure 6.3

Student Tracking Form: Third-grade Reading Targets

	PRACTICE									TEST		
	Synonym / Antonym			Prefix/Suffix			Oral Fluency			Synonym/ Antonym	Prefix/Suffix	Oral Fluency
	(Task #)	(Task #)	(Task #)	(Task #)	(Task #)	(Task #)	(Task #)	(Task #)	(Task #)			
10												
9												
8												
7												
6												
5												
4												
3												
2												
1												
Date												

Learning targets: I can identify synonyms and antonyms.
I can tell the meaning of prefixes and suffixes.
I can read aloud with fluency.

Figure 6.4

Student Tracking Form: Fifth-grade Social Studies Targets

Learning Target	Date	What I did well	What I need to work on
1. I can explain the constitutional structure of our government.			
2. I can describe the processes that have been used to create, amend, and repeal laws.			

work goes home. The information is then available when it is time for students to reflect on their learning and share their progress with others. If you want parents to see these forms, include a place for parent signature and ask students to return them to you or to their learning journal folders. You can also include any daily or weekly reflections (described later in the chapter) in these folders.

You also can have a dedicated book, booklet, or computer file for recording reflections on learning. When you read these journals, you can get insights into how the learning is going and what might be needed in the way of course correction. For example, fourth-grade students at Mark Twain Elementary School in Houston, Texas, make their own journals out of lined paper with construction paper covers. The journals are subject specific and focused on the theme the class is exploring; students record facts and concepts they are learning, describe experiments, pose questions, express opinions, and note insights. Here is how one of the teachers explains why they use journals (Kathleen Blakeslee, personal communication, July 2008):

> The journals provide the students and teachers with regular descriptive feedback. This student feedback guides instruction for the next day. The teachers love reading these journals because they can see what's in students' heads and thereby see the misconceptions and what needs reteaching. As the teachers read the students' journals, they take notes to modify their instruction. The teachers believe that the purpose and success of the journal is its accessibility. It gives everyone a voice, validates every student's thinking because not everyone speaks up in class. It engages students in self-reflection and lets them keep track of and share their learning.

Collecting Samples of Work

Another way for students to track their progress is to keep selected samples of their work in a portfolio. A *portfolio* is simply an intentional collection of artifacts that tell a predetermined story. Common types of portfolios, their purposes, and kinds of artifacts to collect for each are shown in Figure 6.5.

All types of portfolios can be used for self-reflection purposes, but it is important to be clear at the outset what kind of story the evidence is to tell, because that will determine the artifacts you collect. The examples in this chapter will refer to collections documenting growth, completion of a project, and achievement.

Figure 6.5

Portfolio Contents

Type of Portfolio	Purpose	Artifacts to Collect
Growth	To show progress toward one or more learning goals	Artifacts from before, during, and after learning
Project	To document the trajectory of a project	All drafts of work during the creation of the product or performance
Achievement	To demonstrate current level of achievement over a collection of learning targets	Artifacts comprising a representative sample of achievement
Competence	To provide evidence of having attained competence in one or more areas	Artifacts representing highest level of achievement
Celebration	To showcase best work or what the student is most proud of	Student choice based on quality of work or preference

Source: Adapted with permission from R. J. Stiggins, J. A. Arter, J. Chappuis, and S. Chappuis, *Classroom Assessment* for *Student Learning: Doing It Right—Using It Well* (Portland, OR: ETS Assessment Training Institute, 2004), p. 350.

Work samples collected should be dated, and students should know what learning target(s) each sample relates to. Work accompanied solely by a grade or a mark often does not provide enough information for in-depth self-reflecting or explaining achievement to others. To be of maximum use, each sample should show what students have learned or done well and what, if anything, they have yet to learn or need to improve.

You can accomplish this for learning targets students have mastered by having students write the learning target as an "I can" statement and attach it to the work. Or, students can complete a sentence such as one of these:

- My_____ meets these criteria:_____.
- My strengths in this_____ are_____.

With complex learning targets, you may want to use a cover sheet such as one of those shown in Figure 6.6 to capture a more complete description of the learning the artifact demonstrates.

Figure 6.6

Portfolio Contents

Example 1

Date: _____   Title of Selection: _____

Learning target(s) this selection addresses:

What this selection illustrates about my learning:

Why I chose this selection:

Example 2

Date: _____   Name of Assignment: _____

What this shows I am good at/have learned/know how to do:

What this shows I need to work on:

Example 3

Date: _____   Name of Assignment: _____

This shows that I have learned:

Please give special attention to:

Source: Example 1 is adapted with permission from R. J. Stiggins, J. A. Arter, J. Chappuis, and S. Chappuis, *Classroom Assessment* for *Student Learning: Doing It Right—Using It Well: Activities & Resources* CD-ROM (Portland, OR: ETS Assessment Training Institute, 2004), Chapter 12, "Conferences About and with Students."

Students Reflecting on Their Learning

As important as it is, a collection of work does not guarantee reflection will occur. After students (or you) have recorded or assembled the evidence, it's time to have a second look at it. When students engage in self-reflection, they revisit progress made over time, thinking metacognitively about their learning. The difference between self-assessment in Strategy 4 and self-reflection in Strategy 7 is that *self-assessment* centers on reviewing individual pieces of evidence to identify specific strengths and areas for further work, whereas *self-reflection* refers to a more global process of looking back over a collection of evidence. It involves students in drawing conclusions about what they have learned, how they have learned it, what worked and didn't work, what they would do differently, or how far they have come.

Reflecting on Growth

When students reflect on growth, they compare what they used to know or do and what they now know or can do, a process that is more successful when you have made the learning targets clear along the way. It is also helpful if students have evidence (or a record of evidence as described in the previous section) at hand to inform their thinking. The reflection generally includes two parts. The first part makes an assertion of growth and the second part describes the evidence: "I have become better at _____. I used to _____, but now I _____."

Students can state how they have changed in specific or general terms. They can be specific in their assertion by stating one or more learning targets, such as a key understanding, skill, or proficiency: "I have developed a better understanding of major structures of government"; "I have become better at shooting layups"; or "I have become better at explaining similarities and differences." Or, they can make a general statement: "I have become better at volleyball"; "I have become better at drawing"; or "I have become better at math."

A general assertion of change is fine as long as the comparison of previous and current status offers details that support it. Figure 6.7 illustrates what specific supporting evidence could look like with the volleyball example.

You may want to modify the call for evidence to suit your content and students. With younger students, instead of "I used to . . ./Now I . . ." you may ask them to describe (or draw) their "before" picture and their "after picture" (as illustrat-

159

Figure 6.7

Reflecting on Growth: Volleyball

I have become better at _volleyball_

I used to _I didn't use to be able to keep my serves inbound, I wasn't good at serve receive, I didn't like to block._

Now I _can aim my serve. I get low and absorb the force of a serve so I can pass it more accurately. I'm better at jumping to block hits if I'm ever in the front row._

ed in Figure 6.8) and attach samples of their work that match their "before" and "after" descriptions.

Figure 6.9 shows examples of "before" and "after" statements accompanied by short descriptions of the evidence of current status.

Older students can write a paper reflecting on their growth. One way to do this is to have them write a short essay describing what they know about the topic they will be studying at the beginning of the unit or marking period. Keep this essay. At the conclusion of the unit or marking period, ask students to reread it, to consider how their understanding has changed, and to write a second essay describing their growth. For complex learning targets that will be evaluated with a scoring rubric, students can explain their vision of quality at the beginning of the year and then again at the end of the year and compare the two to see how it has changed. The following is an example of an assignment calling for a reflection on growth from a course, "Educational Technology in My Classroom," offered in a teacher preparation graduate program (used with

Figure 6.8

"Before" and "After"

I have become better at ___writing on the lines.___

My "before" picture: ___My letters jumped around.___

My "after" picture: ___They all sit on the line.___

Figure 6.9

FOR EXAMPLE

"Before" and "After" with Evidence

This is my "before" picture	This is my "after" picture	This is my evidence
I am learning to convert fractions to decimals.	I know how to convert fractions to decimals.	This paper shows that I can convert regular fractions like 1/8, improper fractions like 5/4, and mixed numbers like 2 2/3 to decimals.
Inferences: I am learning to make guesses based on clues in what I read.	I can make good inferences. I can make guesses based on clues in what I read.	This is an example of a good inference. I made a guess about why Laurie lied by using clues from the story.
I am learning to write a great lead.	I know how to write a great lead.	In this introduction I have asked a question that gets the reader wondering and sets up my topic. I think the question works because most people wouldn't have thought of it and it gets the reader directed to the focus of what I am going to say.

permission from Damon Osborne, Mount Vernon Nazarene University, Mount Vernon, OH, 2008):

> Reflect on the essay you composed the first class session related to the concept of integrating technology into your classroom. Based on our reading of the text, the assignments, in-class activities, and any additional resources you have encountered over the past several weeks, compare and contrast your current views on how you plan to integrate technology into your classroom. Cite specific tools, websites, and practices that you intend to employ in order to enhance your course content. (n.p.)

The instructor, John Thomas, describes the assignment's effects on his students this way (personal communication, September 2008):

> Without exception, the students had arrived at the end of the course very tired, a little frustrated with the volume of work, and the constant, unrelenting pace of the work resulted in most of the students grumbling. The second assessment of their beliefs and ideas about how they would use technology in their classrooms focused their attention on what they had learned and helped them realize the amount of new information and new knowledge they had acquired. [E]ach student had the same epiphany. For me as the instructor, it was a very powerful assurance of the learning that had taken place during the course.

Figure 6.10 includes excerpts from one student's response. Her remarks reveal the deeper learning that arises from reflecting on how far she has come.

Reflecting on a Project

In addition to reflection on the intended learning targets, complex or challenging projects also offer opportunities for deepened self-awareness and metacognition. Students can document the steps they took and reflect on the effectiveness of their process—what worked and what didn't, and what they would do differently. They can reflect on what they learned about themselves as learners by completing the project. Or, they can reflect on what the project caused them to think or feel about the topic or subject. The following list offers examples of questions to trigger insights generated by the experience of completing a project:

- What steps did you go through to complete this project? Did your process work throughout completion? Did you encounter difficulties? If so, what were they? How did you solve them? What would you do differently next time?

Figure 6.10

Excerpt from a Reflection on Growth in a College Course

After reviewing my essay from the first class I realize how much I have actually learned in class over the past seven weeks. It has not always been evident that I was truly encountering experiences that definitely have to be used in the classroom of today. Today's classroom is so vastly different from the classroom of my childhood and it is different today in comparison to ten years ago. I have seen my view evolve just as the technology has evolved. My first essay was so rudimentary in its content and my understanding of what technology in the classroom is has changed with each and every lesson and assignment. Some of the lessons were overwhelmingly challenging, but once completed showed a wonderful tool that can be used to enhance the lessons to be learned by the students. . . .

[In my initial essay] I mentioned using a microscope and viewing movies as examples of integrating technology into the classroom. The two examples do not even scratch the surface of what is available. As mentioned in Lever-Duffy & McDonald (2008), there are digital technologies . . .

In conclusion I can honestly say that comparing and contrasting my views from eight weeks ago to now has been eye opening. I see it more as a time of growth with technology than as a contrast in viewpoints. . . . I look forward to putting my knowledge to use in the classroom, and now I can appreciate the past eight weeks of anxiety and learning.

Source: Used with permission from Mishell Mueller, unpublished student work, Mount Vernon Nazarene University Adult and Graduate Studies, Mount Vernon, OH, 2008.

- What did you learn about yourself as a learner by doing this project?

- What skills did you develop as a result of doing this project? What skills would you like to develop or refine as a result of doing this project?

- How did your thinking about _____ change as a result of doing this project?

- What impact has doing this project had on your interests regarding _____?

- What did you like most about doing this project? Why? What did you like least? Why?

- What did doing this project teach you about _____?

You can select one for a short reflection or put together a combination and ask students to write a *process paper* that answers those questions. Or, you could let students choose which question or combination of questions to answer in a shorter essay.

Reflecting on Achievement

When students reflect on achievement, they look back over a record (e.g., a completed tracking form) or a collection of their work to identify what they have mastered and what, if anything, they still need to focus on. It is important that the record or collection of work provide clear evidence of what their strengths and needs are. You can use questions such as the following to trigger this kind of self-reflection:

- What did I learn?

- What learning targets have I mastered?

- What are my strengths in this subject?

- What do I still need to work on?

- What learning targets have I not yet mastered?

Reflecting on a record of achievement or a collection of work can also elicit thoughts about the process that led to the achievement. Sometimes this can be even more productive than focusing on the achievement itself or achievement alone. The following are examples of questions you can use to prompt reflection on process:

- What did I learn?

- How did I learn it?

- What would I change about what I did?

- What should I remember to do again?

- What did I learn about myself as a learner?

Students can reflect more generally on their learning over time by responding to a series of prompts: what was interesting, what I have learned, what I am proudest of, and so forth. After you have read the reflections, students can keep them in a learning journal and look back on them to summarize or comment on their learning in preparation for conferences with parents. Figure 6.11 shows an example of a periodic reflection from a middle school social studies class; Figure 6.12 is a weekly reflection from a middle school language arts class. Again, it is helpful if students have access to data or artifacts when completing these forms.

Figure 6.11

FOR EXAMPLE

Reflecting on My Social Studies Achievement

Name: _____

Please complete the following stems with thoughtful responses and complete sentences. You may use your social studies binder to help you review your work so far this year.

So far, this year, I have learned . . .

I still have questions about . . .

I can find answers to these questions by . . .

I need more practice on . . .

My goal for the end of the grading period is . . .

Source: Used with permission from Brenda Doyle, unpublished classroom materials, Olentangy Local Schools, Lewis Center, OH, 2008.

Students Reflecting on Themselves as Learners

Reviewing a record of progress, a series of reflections in a learning journal, a collection of evidence, or a project's artifacts all offer students an opportunity to learn more about themselves. This form of metacognitive thinking involves answering questions such as the following:

- What helps me as a learner?

- What gets in my way as a learner?

- What things are difficult for me as a learner?

- What used to be difficult that is easier now?

- How did that happen?/What did I do to make it happen?

Our students can also profit from self-assessing and reflecting on behavior, work completion, and study habits. In Appendix B you will find a form titled "Reflecting on the First Nine Weeks" that gives an example of what Jessica Cynkar, a sixth-grade language arts teacher, asks her students to do. Here is how

Figure 6.12

FOR EXAMPLE

Weekly Reflection

Week of _____

Three interesting things that I learned this week are:

1.

2.

3.

One thing that I am proudest of in my student notebook this week is:

One thing that I want to improve on next week is:

Next week I want my teacher to do the following:

Source: Used with permission from Jessica Cynkar, unpublished classroom materials, Olentangy Local School District, Lewis Center, OH, 2008.

she describes the benefits of taking the time to have students complete this reflection (personal communication, September 2008):

> By talking with students about their learning and not just about particular projects I felt that I had a clearer picture of my students' learning habits and expectations they set for themselves. The reflections were also useful in helping students set goals for their future learning.

Students Sharing Their Learning

When we think of students sharing their learning, student-led parent-teacher conferences held at the end of a marking period often come to mind. Although they are an effective communication option, if they are not feasible, or if you want students to share in other ways, you have many additional choices, some of which involve face-to-face communication and some of which don't.

Writing to Others

For instance, to communicate with parents, students can write a letter or email message describing what they have mastered or learned or worked on during the week, unit, or marking period. Second-grade teacher Amy Meyer shares how she has set that process up for her students (personal communication, January 2009):

> Every Friday students in my class write a letter to someone at home who will write back to them in their family message journal. When they bring the journal home for the weekend the person at home writes back and these back-and-forth written conversations are all kept in a notebook. The targets change depending on what the kids are working on and then some weeks they glue them in the journal. They check off which ones they have met, then I check off which ones they have met, and then parents and child can look at them when they read the letters. For example, the last couple of weeks the targets have focused on writing a paragraph with a topic sentence and supporting details [Figure 6.13].

Beginning writers might complete a daily calendar of accomplishments and take it home at the end of the week along with their work so they and their parents can talk about their successes at school. Figure 6.14 is an example of a daily calendar designed for primary students.

Figure 6.13

FOR EXAMPLE

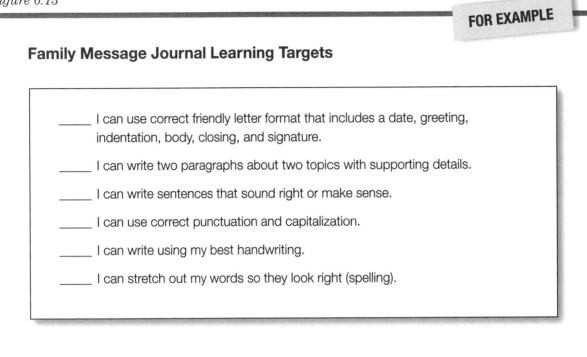

Family Message Journal Learning Targets

_____ I can use correct friendly letter format that includes a date, greeting, indentation, body, closing, and signature.

_____ I can write two paragraphs about two topics with supporting details.

_____ I can write sentences that sound right or make sense.

_____ I can use correct punctuation and capitalization.

_____ I can write using my best handwriting.

_____ I can stretch out my words so they look right (spelling).

Source: Used with permission from Amy Meyer, unpublished classroom materials, Olentangy Local School District, Lewis Center, OH, 2008.

Figure 6.14

FOR EXAMPLE

Look What I Accomplished This Week

	Monday	Tuesday	Wednesday	Thursday	Friday
📖	I read:	I read:	I read:	I read:	I read:
✏️	I wrote:	I wrote:	I wrote:	I wrote:	I wrote:
+ & -	I added and subtracted:	I added and subtracted:	I added and subtracted:	I added and subtracted:	I added and subtracted:

Source: Used with permission from Donna Snodgrass, unpublished classroom materials, Cleveland State University, Cleveland, OH, 2006.

Participating in Conferences

Student-involved conferences can take a number of different forms. Students can conduct a short conference at home with their parents or at school with another student. You can run a handful of student-parent conferences simultaneously in rotating shifts in the classroom during the day, stopping by to check in with each one. You can schedule student-parent-teacher conferences during the marking period or at its conclusion. Parents can come to school to watch and listen as students make presentations. Figure 6.15 lays out the most common permutations. Which one or ones you select will be determined by the kind of information your students are prepared to share and context considerations such as students' ages and the logistics involved.

Inviting Parents to School

When inviting parents to a conference or presentation during the day, it is helpful to give them some time options and ask them to commit to one. Figure 6.16 is an invitation preschool teacher Beth Luengen created to encourage parents to attend their children's project presentations. She reports that both she and another teacher using this form had all students' parents attend, whereas in previous years, using a shorter invitation without the choice of time slots, only one in three students had a parent who came to watch the presentations.

Many teachers report that when students write the invitation to their own parents, attendance increases. It is helpful if parents receive information that lets them know what to expect and offers suggestions for their participation. You can also let parents know how to schedule a separate conference at a different time without their child present, if they wish.

Engaging in a Student-led Conference

Participating in activities drawn from Strategies 1 through 6 will have prepared your students to talk knowledgeably about their growth, their achievement, their strengths, their goals, and their needs as learners. You choose the focus, give students opportunity to reflect on the pertinent artifacts, help them set an agenda for the kind of conference they will be leading, and plan for time for practicing with a peer.

During a student-led conference, typically the student opens by making introductions, if needed, and sharing the agenda. Then the student shares the learning targets or goals that are the focus of the conference and presents and discusses the artifacts selected to illustrate the topic; e.g., growth, achieve-

Figure 6.15

Sharing Options

Purpose: Demonstration of Growth			
Topic	**Artifacts**	**Participants**	**Location**
Improvement on one target	Two or more work samples ("before" and "after")	Student and parent Student and significant adult	Home or school
Growth over time	Collection of work samples Learning journal	Two students Student and teacher Student, parent, and teacher	School

Purpose: Communicating Achievement			
Topic	**Artifacts**	**Participants**	**Location**
Level of achievement or demonstration of competence	Student- or teacher-maintained records Learning journal Collection of work samples Final project Grade report	Student and parent Student and significant adult Two students Student and teacher Student, parent, and teacher	Home or school School
Evidence of meeting goals	Collection of evidence of setting and meeting goals	Student, parent, teacher, other significant adults, community members	

Source: Adapted with permission from R. Stiggins, J. Arter, J. Chappuis, and S. Chappuis, *Classroom Assessment* for *Student Learning: Doing It Right—Using It Well* (Portland, OR: ETS Assessment Training Institute, 2004), p. 364.

Figure 6.16

FOR EXAMPLE

Preschool Parent Invitation

May 27, 2008

Dear Parents,

Your child has been working on an end of the year project and would like to make a personal presentation—just for you! It should only take 15 minutes or so. Please complete this survey and return it to school tomorrow.

❏ I would prefer to come during the school day on Monday, June 2 (between 8:30 and 10:30).

❏ I would prefer to come with my child after school (between 1:30–2:00) this week. Please circle which day you prefer: Thursday or Friday.

❏ I am unable to come to the school. Please send my child's project home at the end of the year.

Thank you for supporting your child's education!

—Mrs. Luengen

Source: Used with permission from Beth Luengen, unpublished classroom materials, Central Oahu School District, Mililani, HI, 2008.

ment, successful completion of a project, competence, attainment of goals, or something else you and your students have chosen. Parents may ask clarifying questions and discuss the work or the learning. Students should think in advance about the kinds of questions their parents may have and be prepared to answer them. The conference closes with the student thanking the parents for coming.

Depending on the type of conference you have selected, you may want to send work samples home in advance for parents to review. Or you and the student may complete a joint report of progress and send that home in advance of a parent conference. Figure 6.17 is an example of a report card completed by both teacher and student, which can form the basis of a student-parent or student-parent-teacher conference. Students can also share with parents the records they have kept, in preparation for or instead of a conference at school.

Figure 6.17

FOR EXAMPLE

GRADE 7 SELF- AND TEACHER EVALUATION

		READING	Trimester 1		Trimester 2		Trimester 3	
K E Y		**5** = Exceeds standards **4** = Meets, and sometimes exceeds, standards **3** = Consistently meets standards **2** = Meets some standards **1** = Does not meet standards	Student	Teacher	Student	Teacher	Student	Teacher
7-1	Word Analysis & Vocabulary	I can use the meaning of parts of a word (prefix, suffix, and root words) to understand the word in text.						
7-2	Comprehension Strategies	I can make connections to what I am reading and I can tell if the connections I am making are helping me to better understand the text.						
7-3		I can figure out the main idea/theme of the text.						
7-4		I can consider information from a variety of texts and judge the value of those ideas.						
7-5		I can make text-to-world and text-to-self connections that increase understanding of the text.						
7-6	Reading Skills	I can summarize or make a short statement of the main points of the text.						
7-7		I can tell the main idea and details in a text.						
7-8		I can develop an accurate summary that includes important ideas from the text as well as my conclusions.						
7-9		I can explain how text features (headings, charts, diagrams, chapter summaries, specialized print, captions, etc.) show the meaning of the text.						
7-10		I can figure out the point of view through the author's language and word choice.						
7-11		I can compare different authors' ideas and opinions about the same event, experience or topic (point of view).						

Source: Used with permission from Jill Meciej, Community Consolidated School District 93, Bloomington, IL, 2008.

Debriefing the Experience

After the conferences, debrief with the class. You can do this formally with a conference evaluation form (Figure 6.18) or informally, using the questions on the conference evaluation form as a discussion guide. You can also ask parents to give you feedback on their experiences using this form.

Figure 6.18

Conference Evaluation Form

| Name: _____ | Date: _____ |

What I learned from this conference	
What I liked about it	
What I would change about the conference	
Other comments	

Source: Adapted with permission from R. Stiggins, J. Arter, J. Chappuis, and S. Chappuis, *Classroom Assessment* for *Student Learning: Doing It Right—Using It Well* (Portland, OR: ETS Assessment Training Institute, 2004), p. 378.

Conclusion

This chapter brings assessment *for* learning full circle. The process of learning awakens glimmerings of self-awareness, which can flit like fireflies around the periphery of our consciousness and then disappear. By giving students structured opportunities to reflect on their learning journey, to capture their observations, and to share them, we can deepen both students' achievement and their insights into themselves as learners.

Closing Thoughts

A secondary foreign language department created an audiotape of each first-year student's initial attempts to speak the language they were studying. At intervals throughout the year students added three-minute segments to their tapes, and at the end of the year they were able to hear the progress they had made. The tapes followed them through their years of foreign language study as they periodically recorded three-minute segments of conversation. The tapes became a portfolio of sorts, a record of growth that students could tune into at any time. And at graduation, the teachers giftwrapped each cassette and presented them to their students.

Assessment *for* learning is a gift we give our students. It is a mirror we hold up to show them how far they have come. It is a promise that we will use assessment, not to punish or reward, but to guide them on their learning journey.

Appendix A
Student-friendly Scoring Rubrics

These three scoring rubrics are offered as examples of what student-friendly language can look like. If you choose to use one of these, first check to see that it aligns with the specific learning targets your students are responsible for mastering.

1. Six-trait Analytical Writing Scoring Guide, Student-friendly Version for Younger Students

2. Central Kitsap School District Scoring Rubric for Mathematics Problem Solving (two versions—one for younger elementary students and one for upper elementary and middle school students)

3. Oral Presentation Scoring Rubric (a single version for middle school and high school students)

For more examples of student-friendly rubrics, see *Creating and Recognizing Quality Rubrics*, by J. Arter and J. Chappuis (Portland, OR: ETS Assessment Training Institute, 2006).

Ideas

—My Message—

5 **READY TO SHARE!**

- It all makes sense. It's really clear.
- My reader will learn a lot.
- This is just what I wanted to say.
- Good, juicy details!

4 *Some of 5, some of 3*

3 **HALFWAY HOME!**

- My reader will get the general idea.
- You might have some questions.
- It TELLS, but doesn't SHOW.
- I need to add some details.
- I'm working on it!

2 *Some of 3, some of 1*

1 **JUST BEGINNING**

- I'm afraid my reader won't follow this.
- It's hard to get started.
- I'm not sure what my topic is . . . OR . . . maybe my topic is TOO BIG.
- The picture is not very clear.
- I need more time to think.

Source: Six-trait Analytical Writing Scoring Guide Student-friendly Version—Younger Students. Adapted with permission from "6+1 Trait™ Writing Assessment Scoring Guide" (Portland, OR: Northwest Regional Educational Laboratory, 1994).

Organization

—from Beginning to End—

5 **READY TO SHARE!**

- I know where I'm going.
- My opening will hook you!
- The ending really works!
- Follow me!
- I see just how all the parts fit together.

4 *Some of 5, some of 3*

3 **HALFWAY HOME!**

- Some pieces of my paper fit better than others.
- My paper is PRETTY easy to follow.
- My beginning is okay.
- Maybe I need to move some things around.
- The ending doesn't grab me yet.

2 *Some of 3, some of 1*

1 **JUST BEGINNING**

- How do I begin? This is confusing!
- What should I tell first?
- What comes next?
- Help! Which pieces go together?
- I don't know where I'm headed.
- How do I end this?

Voice

—Putting MYSELF in My Writing—

5 **READY TO SHARE!**

- It's ME!!! This is what I think.
- I'm speaking right to the reader.
- Hear me ROAR!
- It might make you laugh or cry.
- I love this topic.
- I want my reader to feel what I feel.

4 *Some of 5, some of 3*

3 **HALFWAY HOME!**

- I hear a *little* of me in the writing.
- This topic is OK.
- *Sometimes* I'm speaking to the reader.
- I'm hiding my feelings and ideas a little, but I'm starting to have fun.

2 *Some of 3, some of 1*

1 **JUST BEGINNING**

- I'm not speaking to the reader--*yet.*
- I don't hear myself in this paper.
- This topic is boring.
- SNORE! I wish I didn't have to do this.

Words

—Playing with Language—

5 **READY TO SHARE!**

- My words paint a picture.
- My words make the message CLEAR.
- I love the way my words sound and feel.
- I think this is the BEST way to say it!

4 *Some of 5, some of 3*

3 **HALFWAY HOME!**

- I need more IMAGINATION here!
- These are the first words I thought of.
- Some of the words and phrases are great. Some aren't.
- There is probably a BETTER way to say it.

2 *Some of 3, some of 1*

1 **JUST BEGINNING**

- Some words are really vague.
- These words are NOT my favorites.
- The words I've used don't paint a picture in your mind.
- Some of my words don't make sense to me when I read them over.

Fluency

—Listening to the Sound—

5 **READY TO SHARE!**

- My paper is EASY to read out loud.
- Some sentences are LONG and STRETCHY—some are SHORT and SNAPPY.
- I love the sound of this paper—it's got rhythm!
- My sentences begin in several different ways.

4 *Some of 5, some of 3*

3 **HALFWAY HOME!**

- A lot of my sentences begin the same way.
- I wish my paper sounded a little smoother in places.
- My sentences are all about the same length.
- It's PRETTY easy to read out loud if you take your time.

2 *Some of 3, some of 1*

1 **JUST BEGINNING**

- Help! Some of these sentences don't make sense.
- My paper is HARD to read out loud--even for me!
- Sometimes, I can't tell where to begin a new sentence.
- Everything is strung together in one endless sentence, or there are lots of choppy little sentences, one after another.

Conventions
—Editing—

5 **READY TO SHARE!**

- You have to look hard to find mistakes in my paper!
- I used capitals to **begin sentences** and to indicate **names.**
- My work has been edited and proofread; it's ready to share outside the classroom.
- I checked my spelling.
- I used periods, exclamation points, and question marks in the right spots.

4 *Some of 5, some of 3*

3 **HALFWAY HOME!**

- I'm not sure I spelled all the words right.
- My paper has some mistakes, but you can still read it.
- I might have left out some punctuation.
- I have more editing to do—it's not ready to publish yet.

2 *Some of 3, some of 1*

1 **JUST BEGINNING**

- There are lots of mistakes.
- I have not edited my work.
- It's hard to understand what I'm saying because of spelling or punctuation errors.
- Some things need correcting before I share this.

Mathematical Problem Solving: A Three-trait Model

Central Kitsap School District
Department of Curriculum and Instruction
P.O. Box 8
Silverdale, WA 98383
360-662-1715

Mathematical Knowledge: Concepts and Procedures

Definition: A student demonstrates a grasp of the mathematical concepts, chooses and performs the appropriate mathematical operations, and performs computations correctly.

Problem Solving

Definition: A student demonstrates problem solving skills by showing that he/she understands what the problem asks by framing the problem so that appropriate mathematical process(es) can be selected and used, by developing or selecting and implementing a strategy to find a solution, and by checking the solution for reasonableness.

Mathematical Communication

Definition: A student demonstrates communication skills in mathematics by explaining the steps and reasoning used in a solution process with words, numbers, and/or diagrams.

Source: Both student-friendly versions of this rubric are reprinted with permission from the Central Kitsap School District, Silverdale, WA.

MATHEMATICAL KNOWLEDGE

5 RIGHT ON TARGET!

- I knew what information from the problem to use.

- I knew what operations to use.

- I did all the calculations correctly.

4 *Some of 5, some of 3*

3 ON THE WAY!

- I knew which information to use for part of the problem, but not all of it.

- I knew which operations to use for part of the problem, but not all of it.

- I did some calculations correctly, but I may have made mistakes in some.

2 *Some of 3, some of 1*

1 JUST BEGINNING!

- I wasn't sure what information to use.

- I didn't know what to do with the numbers.

- I didn't understand this problem.

Mathematical Problem Solving Three-trait Model, Younger Student Version

PROBLEM SOLVING

5 RIGHT ON TARGET!

- I knew how to set up the problem.

- The steps I used made it easy to solve the problem.

- I solved the problem.

- My answer fits the question.

4 *Some of 5, some of 3*

3 ON THE WAY!

- I found a way to do the problem, but had to struggle to get an answer.

- My method worked for part of the problem, but not all of it.

- I'm not sure if my answer fits the question.

2 *Some of 3, some of 1*

1 JUST BEGINNING!

- I tried some things, but didn't get anywhere.

- My answer doesn't fit the question.

- I didn't understand this problem.

Mathematical Problem Solving Three-trait Model, Younger Student Version

MATHEMATICAL COMMUNICATION

5 RIGHT ON TARGET!

- I used words, pictures, and numbers to explain what I did and what I was thinking.

- My explanation was clear and organized.

4 *Some of 5, some of 3*

3 ON THE WAY!

- Someone reading my explanation would need more information to understand it.

- I explained the answer, but not how I got it or why my steps work.

2 *Some of 3, some of 1*

1 JUST BEGINNING!

- My explanation is mostly copying the question.

- I'm not sure what my steps were.

- I didn't understand this problem.

Mathematical Problem Solving Three-trait Model, Younger Student Version

MATHEMATICAL CONCEPTS AND PROCEDURES

5 I completely understand the appropriate mathematical operation and use it correctly.

- I understand which math operations are needed.
- I have used all of the important information.
- I did all of my calculations correctly.

4 Some of 5, some of 3

3 I think I understand most of the mathematical operations and how to use them.

- I know which operations to use for some of the problem, but not for all of it.
- I have an idea about where to start.
- I know what operations I need to use, but I'm not sure where the numbers go.
- I picked out some of the important information, but I might have missed some.
- I did the simple calculations right, but I had trouble with the tougher ones.

2 Some of 3, some of 1

1 I wasn't sure which mathematical operation(s) to use or how to use the ones I picked.

- I don't know where to start.
- I'm not sure which information to use.
- I don't know which operations would help me solve the problem.
- I don't think my calculations are correct.

Mathematical Problem Solving Three-trait Model, Student Version

PROBLEM SOLVING

5 **I came up with and used a strategy that really fits and makes it easy to solve this problem.**

- I knew what to do to set up and solve this problem.
- I knew what math operations to use.
- I followed through with my strategy from beginning to end.
- The way I worked the problem makes sense and is easy to follow.
- I may have shown more than one way to solve the problem.
- I checked to make sure my solution makes sense in the original problem.

4 *Some of 5, some of 3*

3 **I came up with and used a strategy, but it doesn't seem to fit the problem as well as it should.**

- I think I know what the problem is about, but I might have a hard time explaining it.
- I arrived at a solution even though I had problems with my strategy at some point.
- My strategy seemed to work at the beginning, but did not work well for the whole problem.
- I checked my solution and it seems to fit the problem.

2 *Some of 3, some of 1*

1 **I didn't have a plan that worked.**

- I tried several things, but didn't get anywhere.
- I didn't know which strategy to use.
- I didn't know how to begin.
- I didn't check to see if my solution makes sense.
- I'm not sure what the problem asks me to do.
- I'm not sure I have enough information to solve the problem.

Mathematical Problem Solving Three-trait Model, Student Version

MATHEMATICAL COMMUNICATION

5 **I clearly explained the process I used and my solution to the problem using numbers, words, pictures, or diagrams.**

- My explanation makes sense.
- I used mathematical terms correctly.
- My work shows what I did and what I was thinking while I worked the problem.
- I've explained why my answer makes sense.
- I used pictures, symbols, and/or diagrams when they made my explanation clearer.
- My explanation was clear and organized.
- My explanation includes just the right amount of detail—not too much or too little.

4 *Some of 5, some of 3*

3 **I explained part of the process I used, or I only explained my answer.**

- I explained some of my steps in solving the problem.
- Someone might have to add some information for my explanation to be easy to follow.
- Some of the mathematical terms I used make sense and help in my explanation.
- I explained my answer, but not my thinking.
- My explanation started out well, but bogged down in the middle.
- When I used pictures, symbols, and/or diagrams, they were incomplete or only helped my explanation a little bit.
- I'm not sure how much detail I need in order to help someone understand what I did.

2 *Some of 3, some of 1*

1 **I did not explain my thinking or my answer, or I am confused about how my explanation relates to the problem.**

- I don't know what to write.
- I can't figure out how to get my ideas in order.
- I'm not sure I used math terms correctly.
- My explanation is mostly copying the original problem.
- The pictures, symbols, and/or diagrams I used would not help somebody understand what I did.

Mathematical Problem Solving Three-trait Model, Student Version

Oral Presentation
Student-friendly Scoring Rubric

Content

- Clear main topic
- All information relates to and supports topic
- Information is important to understanding the topic
- Facts, details, anecdotes, and/or examples make topic come alive for audience

Organization

- Opening introduces topic and catches audience's interest
- Sequence of ideas supports meaning and is easy to follow
- Transition words guide audience
- Conclusion wraps up topic and leaves audience feeling satisfied

Delivery

- Maintains eye contact with audience throughout
- Voice is loud enough for audience to hear
- Articulates clearly
- Speaks at a pace that keeps audience engaged without racing
- Avoids "filler" words ("and," "uh," "um," "you know," "like")
- Uses gestures and movement to enhance meaning
- Uses notes only as reminders
- Visual aids or props, if used, add to meaning

Language Use

- Chooses words and phrases to create a clear understanding of the message
- Uses language techniques (e.g., humor, imagery, simile, and metaphor) effectively as appropriate to topic, purpose, and audience
- Explains unfamiliar terminology, if used
- Matches level of formality in language and tone to purpose and audience
- Uses words and phrases accurately
- Uses correct grammar

Oral Presentation Criterion 1: CONTENT

5: Strong

- My presentation had a clear main topic.

- All of the information in my presentation related to and supported my topic.

- The information I included was important to understanding my topic.

- I chose facts, details, anecdotes, and/or examples to make my topic come alive for my audience.

3: Part-way There

- My topic was fairly broad, but the audience could tell where I was headed.

- Most of my details related to and supported my topic, but some might have been off-topic.

- Some of my information was important, but some details might have been too trivial to be included. Maybe I should have left some details out.

- Some of my information may not have been interesting or useful to my audience.

1: Just Beginning

- I wasn't sure what the focus of my presentation was, or I got mixed up and changed topics during my presentation. I think I wandered through a few topics.

- I didn't really know how to choose details to share, so I just used whatever came into my mind.

- I forgot to think about what information might be most interesting or useful to my audience.

Oral Presentation Criterion 2: **ORGANIZATION**

5: Strong

- The opening of my presentation introduced my topic in a way that caught the audience's interest.

- I chose a sequence for the content of my presentation so that it was easy to follow. My audience could easily make a mental outline of the content.

- I used transition words to guide the audience. I don't think anyone got lost listening to me.

- My conclusion wrapped up my topic and left the audience feeling satisfied.

3: Part-way There

- My presentation had a recognizable opening, but it may have been a little plain.

- Most of my ideas were in an order that's easy to follow, but there may have been a place or two where ideas seemed out of place.

- In some places I may have jumped from one idea to the next without helping the audience follow me.

- I had a conclusion. My audience knew when my presentation was over, but I could have done a better job of leaving them with a feeling of satisfaction.

1: Just Beginning

- I just plunged into my ideas without setting the audience up to hear about my topic.

- I wasn't sure what order to put my ideas in, so they came out in a jumble. I think my audience would have had trouble making a mental outline of the content.

- I left out transitions. I didn't help the audience follow along with my thoughts.

- When I finished, the audience didn't know it was the end. I forgot to make a closing statement.

Oral Presentation Criterion 3: DELIVERY

5: Strong

- I maintained eye contact with the audience throughout my speech.

- My voice was loud enough for the audience to hear.

- I varied my voice level and intonation to emphasize meaning.

- I articulated clearly so the audience was able to understand every word.

- I spoke at a pace that kept the audience engaged without racing through my speech.

- I avoided repeatedly using "filler" words between my ideas (e.g., "and," "uh," "um," "you know," "like").

- I used gestures and movement to enhance the meaning of my words.

- I knew my speech well enough so that I could just glance at my notes to help me remember what to say.

- If I used visual aids or props, they helped make my meaning clearer.

3: Part-way There

- I made eye contact with my audience part of the time. Or, I only made eye contact with a few people in the audience and I forgot to look around at everyone.

- My voice was loud enough for the audience to hear part of the time, but it also was too quiet at times.

- I varied my voice level and intonation a few times to emphasize meaning, but I may have spoken in a monotone part of the time, too.

- I articulated clearly some of the time, but some of the time I mumbled.

- I spoke at a fairly good pace, but there were times when I spoke too quickly.

- Sometimes I used "filler" words between my ideas (e.g., "and," "uh," "um," "you know," "like").

- My gestures and movement might have been a little stiff or unnatural, but they didn't distract the audience from the meaning of my presentation.

- I gave parts of my presentation without having to read my notes, but had to read them quite a bit in places.

- If I used visual aids, they were understandable, but they may not have added much to my meaning.

1: Just Beginning

- I had a hard time making eye contact with my audience. I mostly looked up, away, or down.

- My voice was too quiet for everyone to hear me.

- I may have spoken in a monotone, with no variance in intonation. Or I may have tried to vary my voice level and intonation on certain words, but I wasn't sure which ones to emphasize.

- I mumbled frequently, so the audience had a hard time understanding what I was saying.

- I had a hard time with the speed of my talking—I either raced or dragged through my presentation.

- I used a lot of "filler" words between my ideas (e.g., "and," "uh," "um," "you know," "like").

- My gestures and movement seemed stiff or unnatural, or I moved around so much it distracted the audience from the meaning of my presentation.

- I had to read my notes for most or all of my presentation.

- If I used visual aids, they were confusing. I wasn't sure how to explain them or how to link them to the ideas I was talking about.

Oral Presentation Criterion 4: LANGUAGE USE

5: Strong

- I chose words and phrases that created a precise understanding of my message with the needs of my audience in mind.

- I used language techniques such as humor, imagery, similes, and metaphors effectively as appropriate to my topic, purpose, and audience to enhance my message.

- If I used any vocabulary that was unfamiliar to my audience, I explained it or used it in a context that helped listeners understand the meaning.

- I matched the level of formality in my language and tone to my audience and purpose.

- I used words and phrases accurately.

- My oral presentation was grammatically correct.

3: Part-way There

- In some parts of my presentation the words and phrases I used created a precise understanding of my message. There may have been places where my language did not communicate as clearly as it could have. I may have used some clichés.

- I tried to use language techniques such as humor, imagery, similes, and metaphors as appropriate to my topic, purpose, and audience, but I'm not sure how effective they were in enhancing my message.

- I may have used one or two unfamiliar terms that puzzled my audience.

- My language or tone may have been a little too formal or too casual in places to match the audience or purpose for my presentation.

- I used words and phrases accurately most of the time, but there may have been a few places where I used a word or phrase incorrectly.

- Most of my presentation was grammatically correct. I only had a few problems with usage or syntax.

1: Just Beginning

- Many of my words and phrases were too general to convey meaning precisely. My presentation included a number of clichés. Maybe I'm not sure what it means to use precise language.

- I wasn't sure which language techniques to use. My presentation may have sounded repetitive and dull because I used the same words over and over again.

- I didn't realize (or I forgot) that my audience would not know the meaning of some of the vocabulary I used. I think listeners were confused by my terminology.

- I didn't know how to change my language or tone to match the audience or purpose for my presentation. It was either too formal or too casual.

- I may have used a number of words incorrectly. I just don't know.

- I think I may have made a number of grammar mistakes.

Source: Adapted with permission from J. Arter and J. Chappuis, *Creating and Recognizing Quality Rubrics*, (Portland, OR: ETS Assessment Training Institute, 2006), pp. 244–246.

Appendix B
Reproducible Forms

Appendix B
Table of Contents

The forms in Appendix B may be reproduced for classroom use only.

Stars and Stairs

Name: _____ Date: _____

Name: _____ Date: _____

ETS Assessment Training Institute, 2009.

That's Good! Now This: (Form A)

Name: _____ Date: _____

That's good! _____

_____

_____

_____

_____

Now this: _____

_____

_____

_____

_____

_____

Name: _____ Date: _____

That's good! _____

_____

_____

_____

_____

Now this: _____

_____

_____

_____

_____

_____

ETS Assessment Training Institute, 2009.

That's Good! Now This: (Form B)

Name: _____   Date: _____

MY TEACHER'S COMMENTS:

That's good! _____

_____

_____

_____

_____

Now this: _____

_____

_____

_____

_____

MY COMMENTS:

What I did: _____

_____

_____

_____

_____

_____

Please give special attention to: _____

_____

_____

_____

_____

_____

ETS Assessment Training Institute, 2009.

Assessment Dialogue (Form A)

Name: _____ Date: _____

Assignment: _____ Feedback Focus: _____

MY OPINION

My strengths are _____

_____

_____

What I think I need to work on is _____

_____

_____

FEEDBACK

Strengths: _____

_____

_____

Work on: _____

_____

_____

MY PLAN

What I will do now: _____

_____

_____

_____

_____

_____

_____

_____

ETS Assessment Training Institute, 2009.

Assessment Dialogue (Form B)

Name: _____   Date: _____

Assignment: _____   Feedback Focus: _____

MY OPINION

⭐ My strengths are _____

_____

_____

🪜 What I think I need to work on is _____

_____

_____

MY TEACHER'S FEEDBACK

⭐ Strengths: _____

_____

_____

🪜 Work on: _____

_____

_____

MY PLAN

💡 What I will do now: _____

_____

_____

_____

_____

_____

_____

ETS Assessment Training Institute, 2009.

Peer Response Feedback Sheet

Date: _____

Author: _____

Title: _____

Feedback Requested: _____

My response: _____

_____

_____

_____

_____

Person giving response: _____

Date: _____

Author: _____

Title: _____

Feedback Requested: _____

My response: _____

_____

_____

_____

_____

Person giving response: _____

Learning Chains

cut here to edge of page

Name: _____   Date: _____

I have learned to: _____

_____

Evidence:_____

_____

cut here to edge of page

cut here to edge of page

Name: _____   Date: _____

I have learned to: _____

_____

Evidence:_____

_____

cut here to edge of page

cut here to edge of page

Name: _____   Date: _____

I have learned to: _____

_____

Evidence:_____

_____

cut here to edge of page

Adapted with permission from Donna Snodgrass, unpublished classroom materials, Cleveland State University, Cleveland, OH, 2005.

Stamping Stairs

Name: _____

Learning Target: _____

Success!
Date:

On my way!
Date:

Just beginning!
Date:

Name: _____

Learning Target: _____

Success!
Date:

On my way!
Date:

Just beginning!
Date:

ETS Assessment Training Institute, 2009.

Reviewing My Results

Name: _____ Assignment: _____ Date: _____

Please look at your corrected test and mark whether each problem is right or wrong. Then look at the problems you got wrong and decide if you made a simple mistake. If you did, mark the "Simple Mistake" column. For all the remaining problems you got wrong, mark the "Don't Get It" column.

Problem	Learning Target	Right	Wrong	Simple Mistake	Don't Get It

ETS Assessment Training Institute, 2009.

Analyzing My Results

Name: _____   Assignment: _____   Date: _____

I AM GOOD AT THESE!

Learning targets I got right: _____

_____

_____

_____

I AM PRETTY GOOD AT THESE, BUT NEED TO DO A LITTLE REVIEW

Learning targets I got wrong because of a simple mistake: _____

_____

_____

_____

What I can do to keep this from happening again: _____

_____

_____

_____

I NEED TO KEEP LEARNING THESE

Learning targets I got wrong and I'm not sure what to do to correct them: _____

_____

_____

_____

What I can do to get better at them: _____

_____

_____

_____

ETS Assessment Training Institute, 2009.

Reviewing and Analyzing Results, Secondary Version

Name: _____ Assignment: _____ Date: _____

As you answer each question, decide whether you feel confident in your answer or are unsure about it and mark the corresponding box.

Problem #	Learning Target #	Confident	Unsure		Right	Wrong	Simple Mistake	Don't Get It

Analyzing My Results

1. After your test has been corrected, identify which problems you got right and which you got wrong by putting Xs in the "Right" and "Wrong" columns.

2. Of the problems you got wrong, decide which ones were due to simple mistakes and mark the "Simple Mistake" column. (If it was a simple mistake, you can correct it without help.)

3. For all of the remaining wrong answers, mark the "Don't Get It" column.

ETS Assessment Training Institute, 2009.

Reviewing and Analyzing Results, Secondary Version *(continued)*

Name: _____ Assignment: _____ Date: _____

My Strengths

To identify your areas of strength, write down the learning targets for problems you felt confident about **and** got right.

Learning Target #	Learning Target or Problem Description

My Highest Priority for Studying

To determine what you need to study most, write down the learning targets for problems you marked "Don't Get It" (problems you got wrong, NOT because of a simple mistake).

Learning Target #	Learning Target or Problem Description

What I Need to Review

To determine what you need to review, write down the learning targets for problems you were unsure of and for problems on which you made simple mistakes.

Learning Target #	Learning Target or Problem Description

ETS Assessment Training Institute, 2009.

Stars and Stairs with Evidence

Name: _____   Learning Target: _____

Date:
Evidence:

Date:
Evidence:

Date:
Evidence:

Success!

On my way!

Just beginning!

Name: _____   Learning Target: _____

Date:
Evidence:

Date:
Evidence:

Date:
Evidence:

Success!

On my way!

Just beginning!

ETS Assessment Training Institute, 2009.

Target for Rubric Phrases (Form A)

1   2   3   4

5

I made it!

I'm just beginning.

I can see some progress.

I'm halfway home.

I'm almost there.

ETS Assessment Training Institute, 2009.

Target for Rubric Phrases (Form B)

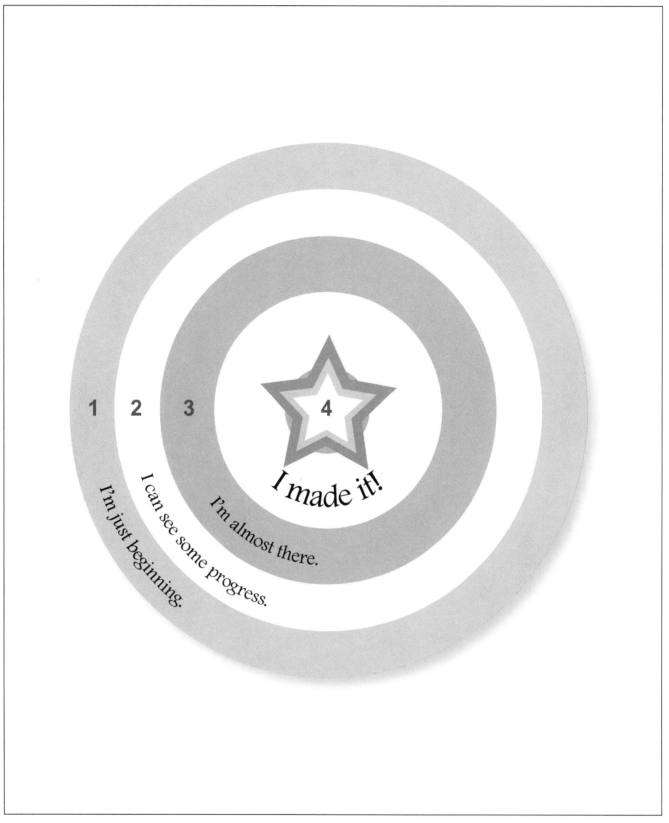

Target for Rubric Phrases (Form C)

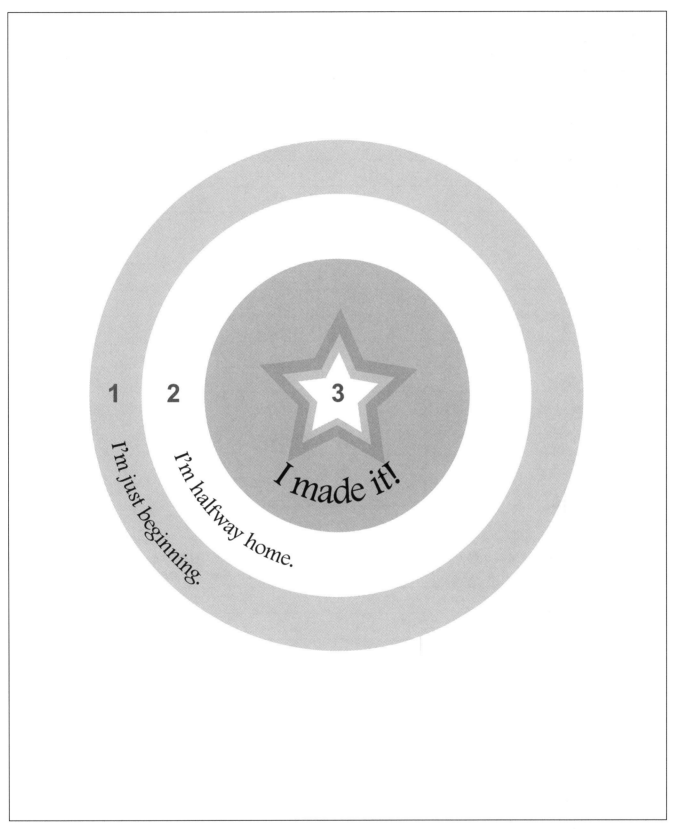

ETS Assessment Training Institute, 2009.

Self-assessment with Rationale

Name: _____ **Date:** _____

Criterion: _____ **My rating:** _____

Rubric phrase that describes my work	Feature of my work that illustrates the phrase

Name: _____ **Date:** _____

Criterion: _____ **My rating:** _____

Rubric phrase that describes my work	Feature of my work that illustrates the phrase

Status, Target, Plan

Name: _____   Date: _____

Status: Right now I can _____

Target: My goal is to _____ by _____

Plan: To reach my goal I will _____

_____

_____

_____

I will get help from _____

Name: _____   Date: _____

Status: Right now I can _____

Target: My goal is to _____ by _____

Plan: To reach my goal I will _____

_____

_____

_____

I will get help from _____

ETS Assessment Training Institute, 2009.

Goal and Plan (Form A)

Name:	Date:
What I need to learn:	
Evidence of current level of achievement:	
Plan of action:	
Help needed—what and who:	
Time frame:	
Evidence of achieving my goal:	

Name:	Date:
What I need to learn:	
Evidence of current level of achievement:	
Plan of action:	
Help needed—what and who:	
Time frame:	
Evidence of achieving my goal:	

ETS Assessment Training Institute, 2009.

Goal and Plan (Form B)

Name: _____ Date: _____

I will learn: _____

My "before" picture—evidence I used to choose my goal: _____

_____

_____

_____

My plan is to: _____

_____

_____

I need these materials: _____

_____

_____

I will ask for help from: _____

I will be ready to show my learning on this day: _____

My "after" picture—I will show my learning by: _____

_____

_____

_____

ETS Assessment Training Institute, 2009.

Goal and Plan (Form C)

Name: _____   Date: _____

Where I Am Going

My goal is to _____

_____

_____

_____

Where I Am Now

Right now, I _____

_____

_____

_____

How I Will Close the Gap

I will meet my goal by doing this: _____

_____

_____

_____

ETS Assessment Training Institute, 2009.

Goal and Plan (Form D)

Name: _____ Date: _____

Learning Target: _____

_____

_____

Current Status: _____

_____

_____

_____

Evidence of Current Status: _____

_____

Plan: _____

_____

_____

_____

_____

Evidence of Achieving My Goal: _____

_____

_____

ETS Assessment Training Institute, 2009.

Goal and Plan (Form E)

Name:	Date:

Where Am I Going?

My goal:

Where Am I Now?

What I can do:	What I need to work on:

How Will I Close the Gap?

- With help from: _____

- Using these materials: _____

- Actions I will take:

   What: _____

   When: _____

ETS Assessment Training Institute, 2009.

Next Steps

Name: _____ Date: _____

Next step for my work:

❏ Get feedback from teacher

❏ Get feedback from another student

❏ Self-assess

❏ Turn in for a grade

❏ Other: _____

_____

_____

_____

Name: _____ Date: _____

Next step for my work:

❏ Get feedback from teacher

❏ Get feedback from another student

❏ Self-assess

❏ Turn in for a grade

❏ Other: _____

_____

_____

_____

ETS Assessment Training Institute, 2009.

Self-assessment and Goal Setting

Name:

Complete this portion at the beginning of an assignment
Learning target I am working on:
Assignment: Date:
Complete this portion after you look at corrections/feedback on your assignment
Strengths:
What to improve:

Name:

Complete this portion at the beginning of an assignment
Learning target I am working on:
Assignment: Date:
Complete this portion after you look at corrections/feedback on your assignment
Strengths:
What to improve:

ETS Assessment Training Institute, 2009.

Correcting Mistakes

Name:	Date:
Learning Target:	
Mistake I made:	Correction:
Mistake I made:	Correction:
Mistake I made:	Correction:
Mistake I made:	Correction:

Name:	Date:
Learning Target:	
Mistake I made:	Correction:
Mistake I made:	Correction:
Mistake I made:	Correction:
Mistake I made:	Correction:

ETS Assessment Training Institute, 2009.

Compare/Contrast (Form A)

Name: _____   Date: _____

When you compare and contrast people, places, objects, or ideas, you are looking for how they are alike and how they are different. One way to organize your information is to use a Venn diagram.

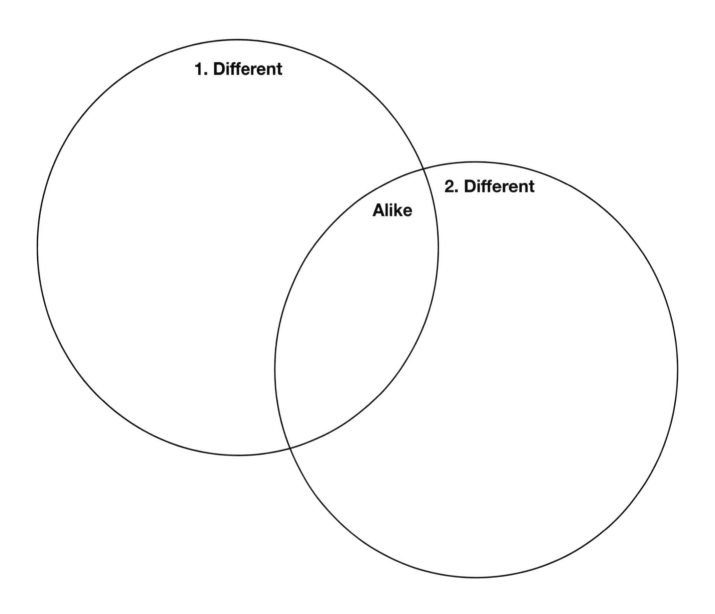

Compare/Contrast (Form B)

Name: _____   Date: _____

When you compare and contrast people, places, objects, or ideas, you are looking for how they are alike and how they are different. One way to organize your information is to use a T-chart. Write details about each thing to be compared in a separate column, then look for similarities and differences.

#1:	#2:

Ways in which they are alike:

Ways in which they are different:

ETS Assessment Training Institute, 2009.

Predictions

Name: _____   Date: _____

To make predictions, use what you already know and clues (from the text, from your observations, etc.) to guess what will happen next.

Page	I predict...	What really happened...

ETS Assessment Training Institute, 2009.

Cause/Effect

Name: _____   Date: _____

When you are figuring out causes and effects, you are looking for a relationship between two or more events. You ask the question, "What happened?" to understand the *effect*. You ask the question, "Why did it happen?" to understand the *cause*.

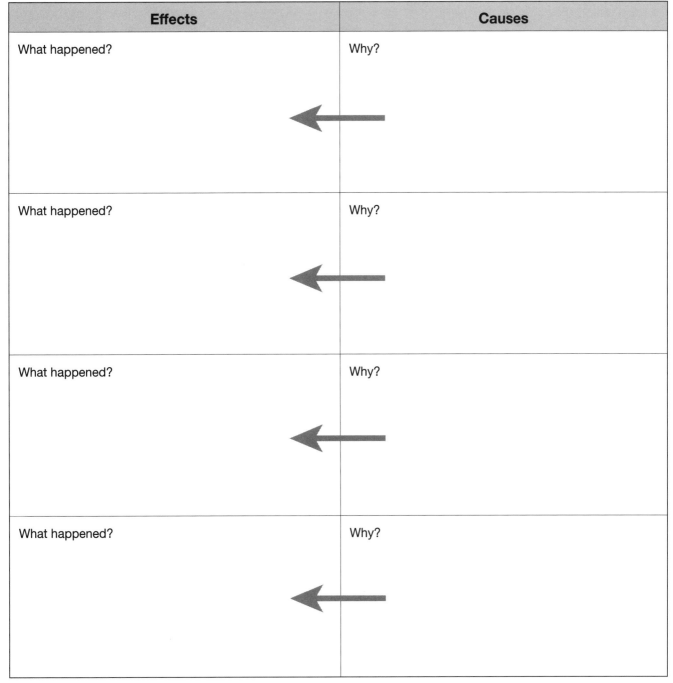

Effects	Causes
What happened?	Why?
What happened?	Why?
What happened?	Why?
What happened?	Why?

ETS Assessment Training Institute, 2009.

Inference

Name: _____   Date: _____

An inference is a reasonable guess based on information. Making an inference is sometimes called "reading between the lines," because the inference is not stated *directly* in the information you have. The information *leads you* to an inference.

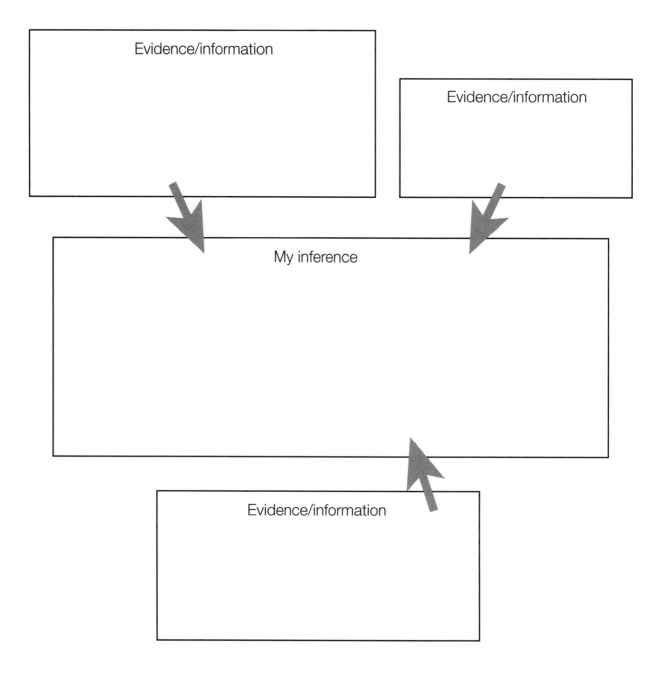

ETS Assessment Training Institute, 2009.

Drawing Conclusions

Name: _____   Date: _____

A conclusion is a special kind of inference. When you draw a conclusion, you begin with a general idea or statement and apply it to a more specific situation. The conclusion applies the information in the general statement to a more specific instance. It often follows the pattern of "if…then," or deductive reasoning.

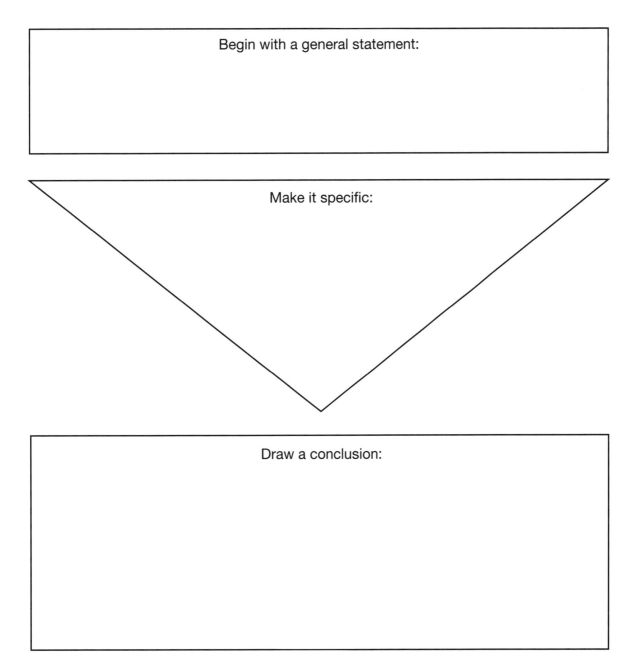

Begin with a general statement:

Make it specific:

Draw a conclusion:

ETS Assessment Training Institute, 2009.

Making a Generalization

Name: _____   Date: _____

When we make a generalization, we compare the pieces of evidence at hand to see what they have in common. Then we make a statement that is true for the pieces of evidence at hand and is also true for a broader array of instances. A generalization is an instance of inductive inference.

Write the commonalities in the outer circles, then make a statement that would apply to the specific examples and also to others like them.

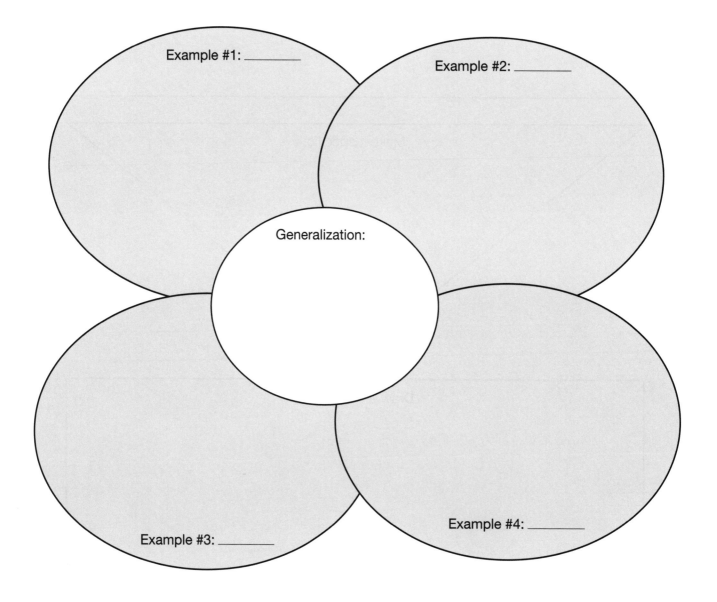

Example #1: _____

Example #2: _____

Generalization:

Example #3: _____

Example #4: _____

ETS Assessment Training Institute, 2009.

Evaluating

Name: _____   Date: _____

Sometimes we compare two things in order to make a judgment. One way to organize your thoughts is to choose categories in which to compare the two things, and then note similarities and differences. You will be able to use this information to support your judgment.

Categories for comparison	#1:	#2:

My judgment:
Reasons for my judgment:

ETS Assessment Training Institute, 2009.

Determining Fact vs. Opinion

Name: _____   Date: _____

A fact is something that can be proved. You could do research to determine whether it is true or false. An opinion is someone's personal idea about something; it cannot be proven true or false. You may agree or disagree with an opinion. When you agree with an opinion, it feels as though it's true, but you cannot prove it's true. That's how you know it's an opinion.

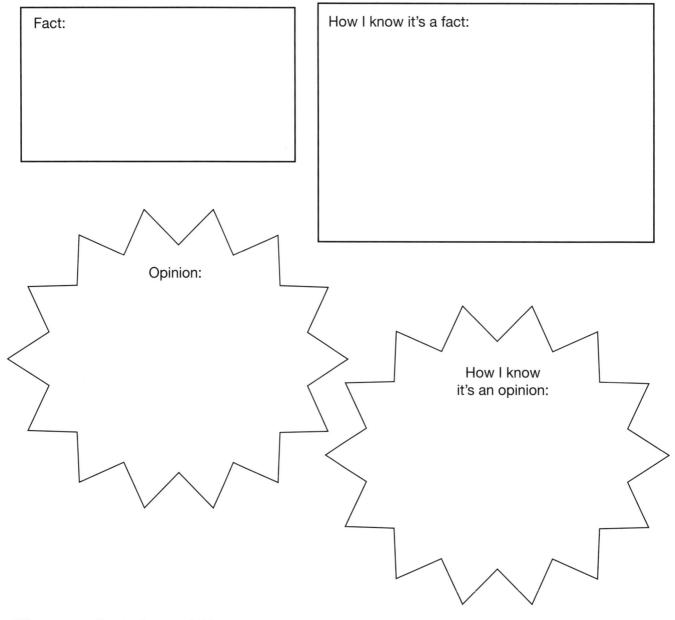

Summary

Name: _____   Date: _____

When you write a summary, you tell the main ideas in your own words.

Main Idea #1
Main Idea #2
Main Idea #3
Main Idea #4

The main ideas in my own words:

Summarize a Plot

Name: _____   Date: _____

First identify the problem and the solution in the story. Next, write a short version of the problem and the solution in your own words.

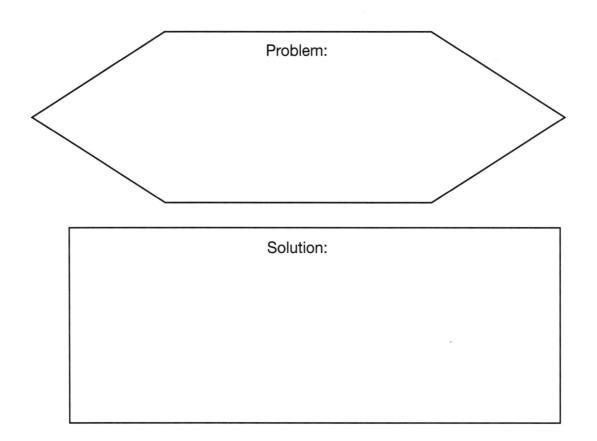

Problem:

Solution:

My summary of the plot:

ETS Assessment Training Institute, 2009.

Main Idea and Supporting Details (Form A)

Name: _____   Date: _____

The main idea is the most important idea in the reading selection. Supporting details tell more about the main idea.

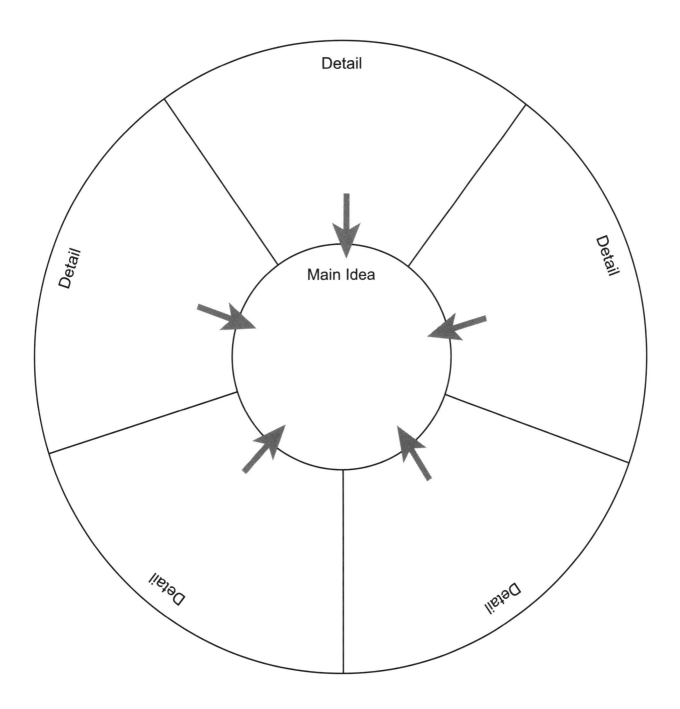

Main Idea and Supporting Details (Form B)

Name: _____   Date: _____

The main idea is the most important idea in the reading selection. Supporting details tell more about the main idea.

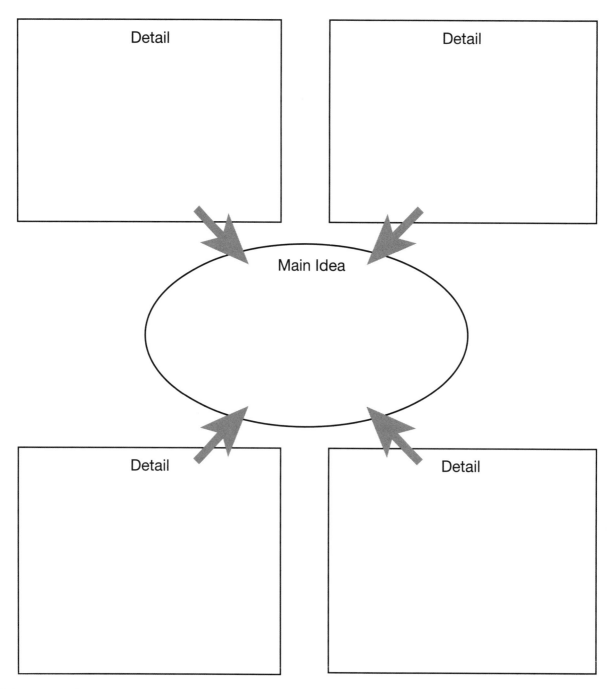

Tracking Progress by Assignment

Name: _____

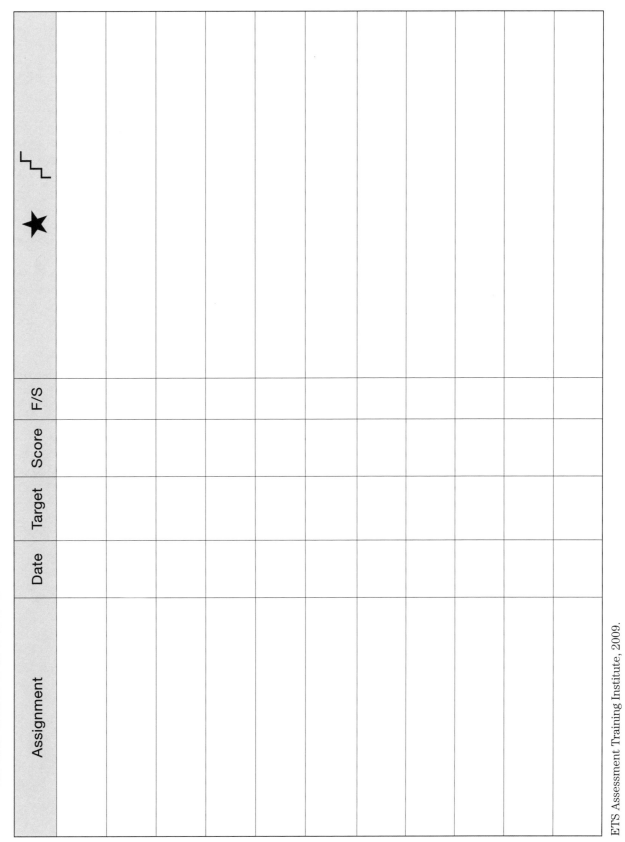

Assignment	Date	Target	Score	F/S	★

Tracking Progress by Learning Targets (Form A)

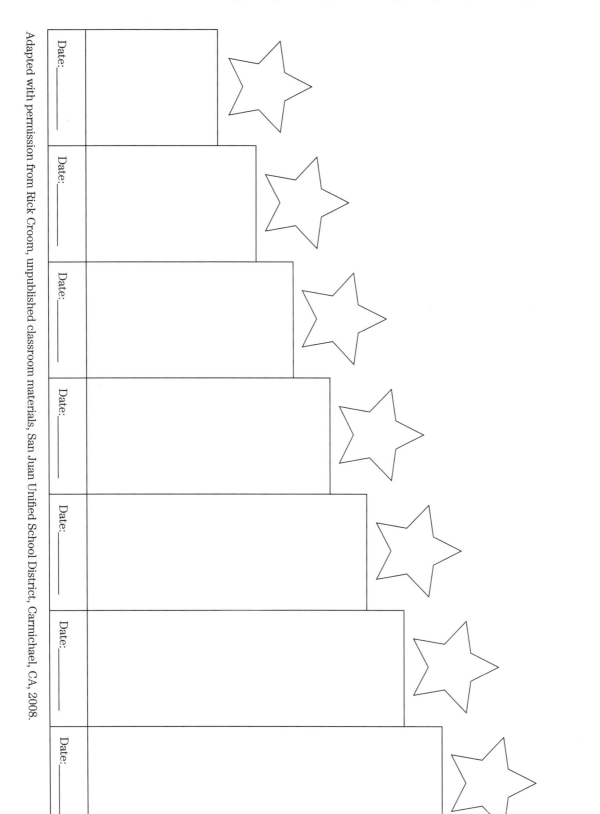

Name: _____

Date: _____

Date: _____

Date: _____

Date: _____

Date: _____

Date: _____

Date: _____

Adapted with permission from Rick Croom, unpublished classroom materials, San Juan Unified School District, Carmichael, CA, 2008.

Tracking Progress by Learning Targets (Form B)

Name: _____

Learning Target	Date	What I did well	What I need to work on

Name: _____

Learning Target	Date	What I did well	What I need to work on

ETS Assessment Training Institute, 2009.

Portfolio Entry Cover Sheet (Form A)

Date: _____   Title of Selection: _____

Learning target(s) this selection addresses:

What this selection illustrates about my learning:

Why I chose this selection:

Date: _____   Title of Selection: _____

Learning target(s) this selection addresses:

What this selection illustrates about my learning:

Why I chose this selection:

ETS Assessment Training Institute, 2009.

Portfolio Entry Cover Sheet (Form B)

Date: _____   Name of Assignment: _____

What this shows I am good at/have learned/know how to do:

What this shows I need to work on:

Date: _____   Name of Assignment: _____

What this shows I am good at/have learned/know how to do:

What this shows I need to work on:

ETS Assessment Training Institute, 2009.

Portfolio Entry Cover Sheet (Form C)

Date: _____   Name of Assignment: _____

This shows that I have learned:

Please give special attention to:

Date: _____   Name of Assignment: _____

This shows that I have learned:

Please give special attention to:

ETS Assessment Training Institute, 2009.

Reflecting on Growth

Name: _____   Date: _____

I have become better at _____

_____

_____

_____

_____

I used to _____

_____

_____

_____

_____

_____

Now I _____

_____

_____

_____

_____

_____

_____

ETS Assessment Training Institute, 2009.

"Before" and "After" with Evidence

Name: _____   **Date:** _____

This is my "before" picture	This is my "after" picture	This is my evidence

Name: _____   **Date:** _____

This is my "before" picture	This is my "after" picture	This is my evidence

ETS Assessment Training Institute, 2009.

Weekly Reflection

Name: _____   Week of _____

Three interesting things that I learned this week:

1. _____

_____

_____

2. _____

_____

_____

3. _____

_____

_____

One thing that I am proudest of in my work this week: _____

_____

_____

One thing that I want to improve on next week: _____

_____

_____

Next week I want my teacher to do the following: _____

_____

_____

Adapted with permission from Jessica Cynkar, unpublished classroom materials, Olentangy Local School District, Lewis Center, OH, 2008.

Conference Evaluation Form

Name: _____   Date: _____

What I learned from this conference	
What I liked about it	
What I would change about the conference	
Other comments	

ETS Assessment Training Institute, 2009.

Reflecting on the First Nine Weeks (page 1)

NAME: _____   DATE: _____

Overall

This grade/class is _____. (harder, easier or about what I expected)

Socialization

The first nine weeks, I socialized:	Too much	Enough	Not enough
The first nine weeks, my parents think I socialized:	Too much	Enough	Not enough

Homework

I complete homework on time in ALL classes.	Yes	No
I check my agenda book AT HOME EVERY night.	Yes	No
I have a comfortable, well-lit place for doing homework.	Yes	No
I have a regular homework time.	Yes	No
I complete my homework before picking up the phone or turning on the TV etc...	Yes	No

Study Habits

The first nine weeks, I studied:	Too much	Enough	Not enough
The first nine weeks, my parents think I studied:	Too much	Enough	Not enough
I typically wait until the night before a test to study.	Yes	No	

Class

I ask questions in class.	Too much	Enough	Not enough
I feel comfortable asking teachers for help.	Yes	No	
I participate in classroom discussions.	Yes	No	

Reflecting on the First Nine Weeks (page 2)

Report Card Reflection

I think I did my best work during the first grading period.	Yes	No
My parents will think I did my best during the first nine weeks.	Yes	No
My teachers think I did my best during the first nine weeks.	Yes	No
My grades represent what I have learned in class.	Yes	No

I learned best when I was able to _____

_____

_____

If I had the quarter to do over again, I would _____

_____

_____

For the second nine weeks, I have decided to _____

_____ so that I'll be more satisfied with my report card.

After reviewing my first nine weeks reflection I have decided that...

My challenge is:

My goal is:

Adapted with permission from Jessica Cynkar, unpublished classroom materials, Olentangy Local School District, Lewis Center, OH, 2008.

Bibliography

Ames, C. 1992. Classrooms: Goals, structures, and student motivation. *Journal of Educational Psychology, 84*(3), 261–271.

Arter, J., & J. Chappuis. 2006. *Creating & recognizing quality rubrics.* Portland, OR: ETS Assessment Training Institute.

Assessment Reform Group. 1999. *Assessment for learning: Beyond the black box.* Cambridge, UK: University of Cambridge School of Education.

Assessment Reform Group. 2002a. Assessment for learning: 10 principles. Retrieved February 10, 2008 from http://www.assessment-reform-group.org.uk

Assessment Reform Group. 2002b. *Testing, motivation and learning.* Cambridge, UK: University of Cambridge, Faculty of Education.

Atkin, J. M., P. Black, & J. Coffey. 2001. *Classroom assessment and the National Science Standards.* Washington, DC: National Academy Press.

Bangert-Drowns, R. L., C-L. C. Kulik, J. A. Kulik, & M. T. Morgan. 1991. The instructional effect of feedback in testlike events. *Review of Educational Research, 61*(2), 213–238.

Bennett, N., & J. Kell. 1989. *A good start? Four year olds in infant schools.* Oxford, UK: Blackwell.

Black, P. 2003a. Formative and summative assessment: Can they serve learning together? Paper presented at the American Educational Research Association annual meeting, Chicago, IL, April 23.

Black, P. 2003b. The nature and value of formative assessment for learning. Paper presented at the American Educational Research Association annual meeting, Chicago, IL, April 22.

Black, P. 2003c. A successful intervention—why did it work? Paper presented at the American Educational Research Association annual meeting, Chicago, IL, April 24.

Black, P., C. Harrison, C. Lee, B. Marshall, & D. Wiliam. 2002. *Working inside the black box: Assessment for learning in the classroom.* London: King's College Press.

Black, P., & D. Wiliam. 1998a. Assessment and classroom learning. *Assessment in Education (5)*1, 7–74.

Black, P., & D. Wiliam. 1998b. Inside the black box: Raising standards through classroom assessment. *Phi Delta Kappan, 80*(2), 139–148.

Blackwell, L., K. Trzesniewski, & C. Dweck. 2007. Implicit theories of intelligence predict achievement across an adolescent transition: A longitudinal study and an intervention. *Child Development, 78*(1), 246–263.

Bloom, B. 1984. The search for methods of group instruction as effective as one-to-one tutoring. *Educational Leadership, 41*(8), 4–17.

Boston, C. 2002. The concept of formative assessment. *ERIC Digest.* College Park, MD: ERIC Clearinghouse on Assessment and Evaluation.

Broadfoot, P. 2007. *An introduction to assessment.* York, UK: Continuum International.

Brookhart, S. M. 1995. Effects of the classroom assessment environment on achievement in mathematics and science. Paper presented at the American Educational Research Association annual meeting, San Francisco, April 18–22.

Brookhart, S. M. 2001. Successful students' formative and summative uses of assessment information. *Assessment in Education, 8*(2), 153–169.

Brookhart, S. M. 2004a. Classroom assessment: Tensions and intersections in theory and practice. *Teachers College Record, (106)*3, 429–458.

Brookhart, S. M. 2004b. *Grading.* Upper Saddle River, NJ: Pearson Education.

Brookhart, S. M., M. Andolina, M. Zuza, & R. Furman. 2004. Minute math: An action research study of pupil self-assessment. *Educational Studies in Mathematics, 57,* 213–227.

Brookhart, S. M., & D. Bronowicz. 2003. "I don't like writing. It makes my fingers hurt": Students talk about their classroom assessments. *Assessment in Education, 10*(2), 221–242.

Brookhart, S. M., & J. DeVoge. 1999. Testing a theory about the role of classroom assessment in student motivation and achievement. *Applied Measurement in Education, 12*(4), 409–425.

Brookhart, S. M., & D. Durkin. 2003. Classroom assessment, student motivation, and achievement in high school social studies classes. *Applied Measurement in Education, 16*(1), 27–54.

Brown, A. 1994. The advancement of learning. *Educational Researcher, 23*(8), 4–12.

Butler, R. 1988. Enhancing and undermining intrinsic motivation: The effects of task-involving and ego-involving evaluation on interest and performance. *British Journal of Educational Psychology, 58,* 1–14.

Butler, R., & O. Newman. 1995. Effects of task and ego-achieving goals on help-seeking behaviours and attitudes. *Journal of Educational Psychology, 87*(2), 261–271.

Cameron, C., B. Tate, D. McNaughton, & C. Politano. 1997. *Recognition without rewards.* Winnipeg, MT: Peguis.

Cameron, J., & D. P. Pierce. 1994. Reinforcement, reward, and intrinsic motivation: A meta-analysis. *Review of Educational Research, 64*(3), 363–423.

Campbell Hill, B., & C. Ruptic. 1994. *Practical aspects of authentic assessment: Putting the pieces together.* Norwood, MA: Christopher Gordon.

Chappuis, J. 2005. Helping students understand assessment. *Educational Leadership 63*(3), 39–43.

Chappuis, S., & J. Chappuis. 2008. The best value in formative assessment. *Educational Leadership 65*(4), 14–18.

Chappuis, S., J. Chappuis, & R. Stiggins. 2009. Supporting teacher learning teams. *Educational Leadership 66*(5), 56–60.

Chappuis, S., R. Stiggins, J. Arter, & J. Chappuis. 2004. *Assessment* for *learning: An action guide for school leaders.* Portland, OR: ETS Assessment Training Institute.

Charleton, B. C. 2005. *Informal assessment strategies.* Markham, ON: Pembroke.

Clarke, S. 1998. *Targeting assessment in the primary classroom.* London: Hodder Murray.

Clarke, S. 2003. *Enriching feedback in the primary classroom.* London: Hodder Murray.

Clarke, S. 2005. *Formative assessment in action: Weaving the elements together.* London: Hodder Murray.

Costa, A. L., & B. Kallick. 2004. *Assessment strategies for self-directed learning.* Thousand Oaks, CA: Corwin.

Crooks, T. 2001. The validity of formative assessments. Paper presented at the 2001 Annual Meeting of the British Educational Research Association, Leeds, UK, September 13–15.

Davies, A. 2000. *Making classroom assessment work.* Merville, BC: Connections.

Davies, A., C. Cameron, C. Politano, & K. Gregory. 1992. *Together is better: Collaborative assessment, evaluation & reporting.* Winnipeg, MT: Peguis.

Davies, A., & K. Busick, eds. 2007a. *What's working in high schools? Book one.* Courtenay, BC: Connections.

Davies, A., & K. Busick, eds. 2007b. *What's working in high schools? Book two.* Courtenay, BC: Connections.

Dweck, C. S. 2001. *Self-theories: Their role in motivation, personality, and development.* Philadelphia: Psychology Press.

Dweck, C. S. 2006. *Mindset: The new psychology of success.* New York: Random House.

Dweck, C. S. 2007. The secret to raising smart kids. *Scientific American Mind,* November 28, 2007. Retrieved November 12, 2008 from http://www.sciam.com/article.cfm?id=the-secret-to-raising-smart-kids&print=true

Earl, L. M. 2003. *Assessment as learning: Using classroom assessment to maximize student learning.* Thousand Oaks, CA: Corwin.

Eisenberger, J., M. Conti-D'Antonio, & R. Bertrando. 2005. *Self-efficacy: Raising the bar for all students*, 2nd ed. Larchmont, NY: Eye on Education.

Elawar, M., & L. Corno. 1985. A factorial experiment in teachers' written feedback on student homework: Changing teacher behavior a little rather than a lot. *Journal of Educational Psychology, 77*(2), 162–173.

Gregory, K., C. Cameron, & A. Davies. 1997. *Knowing what counts: Setting and using criteria.* Merville, BC: Connections.

Gregory, K., C. Cameron, & A. Davies. 2000. *Knowing what counts: Self-assessment and goal-setting.* Merville, BC: Connections.

Hanson, J. 1998. *When learners evaluate.* Portsmouth, NH: Heinemann.

Harlen, W. 2007. Formative classroom assessment in science and mathematics. In J. H. McMillan (ed.), *Formative classroom assessment: Theory into practice* (pp. 116–135). New York: Teachers College Press.

Harlen, W., & M. James. 1997. Assessment and learning: Differences and relationships between formative and summative assessment. *Assessment in Education: Principles, Policy, & Practice 4*(3), 365–379.

Hattie, J., & H. Timperley. 2007. The power of feedback. *Review of Educational Research.* Retrieved October 9, 2007 from http://rer.sagepub.com

Heritage, M. 2007a. Formative assessment: What do teachers need to know and do? *Phi Delta Kappan, 89*(2), 140–145.

Heritage, M. 2007b. *Learning progressions: Supporting instruction and formative assessment.* Paper prepared for the Formative Assessment for Students and Teachers (FAST) State Collaborative on Assessment and Student Standards (SCASS). Washington, DC: Council of Chief State School Officers.

Hunter, M. 1982. *Mastery teaching: Increasing instructional effectiveness in elementary, secondary schools, colleges and universities.* El Segundo, CA: TIP Publications.

Kluger, A. N., & A. DeNisi. 1996. The effects of feedback interventions on performance: A historical review, a meta-analysis, and a preliminary feedback intervention theory. *Psychological Bulletin, 119*(2), 254–284.

Marzano, R., D. Pickering, & J. McTighe. 1993. *Assessing student outcomes: Performance assessment using the dimensions of learning model.* Alexandria, VA: Association for Supervision and Curriculum Development.

McMillan, J. H., ed. 2007. *Formative classroom assessment: Theory into practice.* New York: Teachers College Press.

Morgan, A. 2008. *Feedback: Assessment for, rather than of, learning.* Retrieved September 3, 2008 from http://www.bangor.ac.uk/adu/the_scheme/documents/FEEDBACKJanuary06_000.ppt

National Research Council. 1996. *National science education standards.* Washington, DC: National Academy Press.

Natriello, G. 1987. The impact of evaluation processes on students. *Educational Psychologist, 22*(2), 155–175.

Northwest Regional Educational Laboratory. 1999. *Seeing with new eyes: A guidebook on teaching and assessing beginning writers.* Portland, OR: Author.

Rea-Dickins, P. 2001. Mirror, mirror on the wall: Identifying process of classroom assessment. *Language Testing, 18,* 429–462.

Sadler, D. R. 1989. Formative assessment and the design of instructional systems. *Instructional Science, 18,* 119–144.

Sadler, D. R. 1998. Formative assessment: Revisiting the territory. *Assessment in Education, 5*(1), 77–84.

Shepard, L. A. 2000. The role of assessment in a learning culture. *Educational Researcher, 29*(7), 4–14.

Shepard, L. A. 2001. The role of classroom assessment in teaching and learning. In V. Richardson (ed.), *Handbook of research on teaching,* 4th ed. (pp. 1066–1101). Washington, DC: American Educational Research Association.

Shepard, L. A. 2005. Linking formative assessment to scaffolding. *Educational Leadership, 63*(3), 66–70.

Shepard, L. A. 2008. Formative assessment: Caveat emptor. In C. Dwyer (ed.), *The future of assessment: Shaping teaching and learning* (pp. 279–303). New York: Lawrence Erlbaum Associates.

Shute, V. J. 2007. *Focus on formative assessment.* (ETS Report No. RR-07-11). Princeton, NJ: Educational Testing Service.

Spandel, V. 2009. *Creating writers through 6-trait writing assessment and instruction.* Boston, MA: Pearson.

Stiggins, R. 2007. Assessment for learning: An essential foundation of productive instruction. In Douglas Reeves (ed.), *Ahead of the curve* (pp. 59–76). Bloomington, IN: Solution Tree.

Stiggins, R., J. Arter, J. Chappuis, & S. Chappuis. 2004. *Classroom assessment* for *student learning: Doing it right—Using it well.* Portland, OR: ETS Assessment Training Institute.

Suffolk County Council. 2001. *"How am I doing?"—Assessment and feedback to learners.* Ipswich, UK: Suffolk County Council. Retrieved August 24, 2008 from http://www.slamnet.org.uk/assessment/Hengrave%20site/howamIdoing.pdf

Tomlinson, C. A. 1999. *The differentiated classroom: Responding to the needs of all learners.* Alexandria, VA: Association for Supervision and Curriculum Development.

White, B. Y., & J. R. Frederiksen. 1998. Inquiry, modeling, and metacognition: Making science accessible to all students. *Cognition and Instruction, 16*(1), 3–118.

Wiggins, G. 1998. *Educative assessment: Designing assessments to inform and improve student performance.* San Francisco: Jossey-Bass.

Wiliam, D., & S. Leahy. 2007. A theoretical foundation for formative assessment. In J. H. McMillan (ed.), *Formative classroom assessment: Theory into practice* (pp. 29–42). New York: Teachers College Press.

Wiliam, D., & C. Lee. 2001. Teachers developing assessment for learning: Impact on student achievement. Paper presented at the 27th annual conference of the British Educational Research Association, University of Leeds, September.

Wlodkowski, R. J., & J. Jaynes. 1990. E*ager to learn: Helping children become motivated and love learning.* San Francisco: Jossey-Bass.

Zimmerman, B. 2008. Investigating self-regulation and motivation: Historical background, methodological development, and future prospects. *American Educational Research Association Journal, 45*(1), 166–183.